the problem
with women...
is Men

Cover art by Adam Oslund

Illustrations by Pablo Gonzalez

ISBN: 1-4392-0514-0
ISBN-13: 9781439205143

More information can be found online at
theproblemwithwomenismen.com

the Problem with Women... is Men

The Evolution of a "Man's Man" to a Man of Higher Consciousness

Charles J. Orlando

Dedicated to my loving wife, Tina. Without you I would not be the man I am today. Thank you for your patience, understanding, and wisdom. I love you. And I'll admit it to millions: Honey, you're a better driver than I.

To Jordan and Drew—our incredibly bright and loving kids: You are so cool, so much fun, and so full of life. If I had just one wish for you, it would be for you to follow our example, and choose a significant other with whom you can be happy. Everything after that is gravy.

To my dear mother, Kharyn Leigh: Mom, this would not have come to fruition without your guidance and insights, both now and in my childhood. Thank you so much.

Table of Contents

Disclaimer

Although the techniques I have presented here have worked for many people, they may not work for all. Please use your discretion before trying any of these techniques in your own relationship or situation. The author assumes no responsibility for any perceived positive or negative result of having read the information offered herein.

There were 1,197 female and 381 male participants in this study. To protect their identities, names and any identifying features of all people mentioned in this book have been changed.

Introduction

The *Problem with Women... is Men* is a journey into the minds and real-world experiences of hundreds of men, women, and... me—a recovered playboy, now married with a family, my eye firmly set on becoming a better man/ human being. And what a journey it's been—figuratively and literally. I was of the humble opinion that I knew a lot about the opposite sex (cough!), but I don't think anything would have prepared me for learning about the *true* inner workings of women—their wants, desires, and frustrations. And I certainly wasn't ready to observe how men seem to purposefully keep women down/back/under their thumbs in their quest for control.

Women in committed relationships are looking for meaningful guidance to help them in making their relationships healthier and happier. They are way past the point of reading books giving them some basic dating do's and don'ts the world's "relationship experts" have afforded them to date. Women want to understand men and their issues, to be sure; but they are also looking to improve the quality of their relationships while staying empowered—as women. To that end, this book is written not only from a

NOTES

man's perspective, but also from an enlightened Evolved Man's point of view—a man who has embraced his shortcomings, done the work, and grown as a human being. My hope is for you, the Reader, to experiment with some of the possible solutions presented, to see the difficulties from a different perspective, and to learn how to establish a healthy relationship. If you are a man, this book should serve you as a very important wake-up call, and potentially start you on an Evolutionary path to better yourself and your relationships. If you are a woman, you will be provided with crucial insider-information regarding the frustrations and problems you experience in your romantic relationships...as well as some direct-from-the-source techniques on how to alter your thinking on dealing with men.

So, how did all of this come to pass? I've done a lot of listening and observing—two crucial skills that are major stumbling blocks for most men: Ten years of informal, anecdotal observation, hundreds of interviews with both men and women over the course of three years, and a number of months of quasi-formal research. It's been fascinating. I connected with people across a wide variety of economic, ethnic, and educational backgrounds, for the express purposes of discussing the problems women face with men, as well as the issues men experience themselves. Conversations took place in a variety of unique settings—on commuter trains, in coffee shops, on airplanes, online in organized focus groups, and in internet chatrooms. The informality inherent in these settings paved the way for honest, candid discussions I've found to be lacking in many of the studies I've been exposed to. I spoke with women who were tired of being treated "like a sexual doormat" (so said Angie in Wichita), and with men who—among other issues—were tired of being accused of being gay "...because I enjoy shopping, and find doing laundry therapeutic," (as Steve in Boston said, clearly frustrated). Steve was far from alone in his feelings, and statements like his were very much a concern to me. The last

NOTES

time I checked, I hadn't found shopping or doing laundry to be homosexual activities, but rather *life necessities*. And Angie's declaration was just the tip of the iceberg regarding the plethora of frustrations women passionately vented to me. Over the course of these interviews, it became painfully obvious that Angie, Steve, and hundreds of other men and women had been waiting with bated breath to speak with someone who would finally give them true insights into the roadblocks to happy and healthy relationships. I sat in awe, in the truest sense of the word. My interviewees—veritable strangers—completely bore their souls and psyches, and laid bare their personal relationships for open discussion—clearly relieved that a man was willing to listen.

The majority of the interviews were with women. During our time together, I was in effect, one of the girls. Based on my experiences, newfound knowledge, and *listening skills*, I was able to truly identify with their frustrations—to honestly see what they saw and felt—in their relationships. Perhaps for the first time, these women felt vindicated. They explained to me how they want their partner to talk *with them*, not talk *at them*. They want to be listened to, not merely heard. They want to be emotionally connected to their partner as equals in the relationship. Some women were unmarried, but in a committed relationship at the time they participated in the study. Others were married, some with and some without children. From the stay-at-home mom of 25+ years to the advertising executive who clears $2.5M annually, they all were facing the same sanity-testing issues in their romantic relationships. As we spoke, we reached a silent accord: They would vent and share the personal details of their relationships and lives, and I would—without a hint of judgment—listen and offer solace. But my most important contribution would be to provide them with hard-won insights from my life experiences; those of a man who has been on both sides of the tracks—a rogue playboy, turned upstanding gentleman.

NOTES

Full disclosure: I am not an accredited expert on relationships. If you are reading this with expectations of reviewing data gathered from years of clinical trials or double-blind research studies, or of reading advice from an MBA graduate who based his thesis on the problems and cures for troubled relationships, this book may not be for you. What you are about to read is a combination of research and experiences—both from my own life, and from the lives of others. I wrote this book in the hopes of achieving two goals: 1) to help men Evolve to a better place; and 2) to help women improve their romantic relationships, and face their own issues regarding self-empowerment.

Truth be told, I do come from the shadier side of romantic relationships. However, an epiphany at age 25 led to a period of deep introspection. Over time, I finally realized that, yes... I had chosen the path to sex... not to love, trust, sharing and intimacy. After all, a man who practices deception and emotional coercion in order to selfishly usher a women into bed isn't really on a path to anywhere that's meaningful (at least in the long-term). With my new awareness and strong desire to change and grow emotionally, I looked for guidelines that might point the way to my transformation. Unfortunately, there was no established course to maturity for men of my mindset. As such, I was forced to create one—a path built on honor, mutual respect, sincere and non-defensive listening, civility, honest communication, emotional availability, and a general thoughtfulness. It is through my past and present experiences—coupled with my research—that I have come to a forward-thinking conclusion: Men—in all their remote-clicking, control-hoarding, unkempt-hair wearing glory—need to rise from their passive-aggressive/mixed message-sending ashes, and answer the call of the woman in their lives... a call for understanding, listening, support, happiness... and equality.

The initial impetus for writing this book came from a single thought that plagued me relentlessly: To whom will

NOTES

our ten-years-young daughter pledge her love and life in the future? I realize that I'm asking this question prematurely. And yet, when looking at the *selection*—if you will—of her potential suitors, I find the possible choices increasingly disconcerting. My fervent hope is that she has paid attention to the relationship I have with her mother—my lover, wife, confidante, and best friend—and will wait patiently for a true *partner* to join her in her life, not just a mate for the sake of marriage.

Growth and introspection aside, I'm not entirely sure where my mindset emanates from. In speaking with my mother, we found that she had no real insights, as neither of my parents reflect my attitude toward relationships and romance. She feels her father loved her, but was emotionally unavailable, relating by way of sending messages through her mother—as opposed to establishing an honest, direct relationship with his daughter. As she was growing up, there were no family conversations at all regarding parental opinions/guidance concerning her life goals, nor were any thoughts ever spoken or solicited concerning her friendships/relationships with young people.

My father (now passed) was a kind, good-hearted man whose love for me knew no bounds. As an adult, I can see the downside of it: He was incapable of setting healthy parental limits for me as I was growing up. Looking back on my parents' marriage (which ended when my mother filed for divorce when I was four), I see my father's behavior as quintessentially passive-aggressive. Fortunately I didn't emulate that characteristic, nor was it genetically passed down to me.

There weren't any healthy role models during my adolescence, and I entered adulthood stumbling toward/working at gradually forging a new life path on uncharted territory. As I continued the struggle of finding out more of what my inner core was all about, I made a very surprising

NOTES

discovery: I realized that I found typical male behavior absolutely appalling: rude, condescending, obnoxious, bull-headed, and selfish. Through my transition and Evolution, I have learned that I'm nothing like the stereotypic man. I look at these men and cannot fathom the idea of having even an acquaintanceship—let alone a real friendship—with most of them. To add insult to injury, my newfound views had led some people (including long-time friends) to wonder what my "label" was:

- "Is he 'straight'?"

- "He has homosexual tendencies."

- "He must be in the closet. You watch. He'll be 'out' in 10 years when he leaves his wife for a man."

Contrary to these shortsighted, ignorant statements, I have never been confused about my sexual orientation. I am a straight man, but I'm not the stereotypic "Man's Man" I've described. I mean, since when does actively listening to your wife and being dedicated to her success and happiness equate to homosexuality? And, from that misguided notion, shall we infer that all homosexuals/lesbians have the crucial listening/feeling skill-sets that make for long-lasting healthy egalitarian relationships that straight folks don't have? Just a rhetorical question; the answer is a no-brainer. People who are gay have some of the same problems in their relationships as straight people have (but that is a matter better addressed in a different book).

Regardless, I sympathize *completely* with women today, as I cannot imagine having to choose one of these losers! I'm not an activist for any present-day women's temperance movement, but when you look at the average man, what do you see? Belching, beer-drinking, farting, scratching and picking at various parts of his anatomy, power-watching ESPN. Although too out of shape to play the game, he's

NOTES

always coordinated enough to hit the remote to cheer "his team" on —all the while wearing a belt around/under his beer belly that's so tight it looks like it's hanging on for dear life. *This* is the vision of my future son-in-law? (Note: I'm fully aware that not all men exhibit all of these traits, but behaviors such as these abound in the average man.)

As of late, a New Age buzzword has emerged to describe men for whom my description of the average man does not apply: metrosexual. According to the media, these men are—may the gay/lesbian communities forgive me for even quoting this media madness—"gay men in-training" who, in addition to having style and culture, supposedly carry themselves effeminately, get manicures, and carry a "man purse." What nonsense. Men with honor and class are beyond the labels of *gay* and *straight*. Besides, the mere fact that a man of pride and emotional availability would have to be labeled as a watered-down version of a man (read: man-light) shows a huge disconnect between my sense of masculinity, and what society defines as manly. If caring about my appearance, my family, and myself is gay… then call me "gay." I really couldn't care less.

To help women tackle the well-known problems they have with men, there are a number of popular TV shows, websites, newsletters, and self-help books that attempt to discuss what men are all about, and purport to help women understand men better. When I reviewed a number of these marketing-infused offerings, I found they share striking similarities:

1. Women write the majority of these self-help tomes, so a man's perspective on *his* thoughts and actions is conspicuously missing. In my opinion (and with no disrespect intended toward those female writers), it doesn't matter how a woman analyzes and assesses men's societal ills, or how many focus groups she

NOTES

holds; she is still *not a man*... and she never will be. She is attempting to interpret men; her data-driven research is internalized and offered solely from a woman's point of view, and thus incomplete. There is no choice but for her views to be skewed, because they're based on the following societal program: Women are responsible for the problems in relationships, and must fix them (more on this later).

2. Most books of this genre tend to be written from one of two perspectives:

   - Dating Advice: "Here are a number of cute anecdotes about what men really mean when they don't respond to your telephone messages, or don't call for two weeks after you go on a date with them."

   - Clinical: "A man who calls his mother on a daily basis clearly has Freudian issues concerning separation, codependency, and an over-developed desire to please..." blah, blah, blah...

3. The majority of these self-help books are women's survival guides, and focus on their own self-improvement. In other words, how a woman can *change herself* in order to survive in a relationship with a man and his unresolved issues.

The basic premise of these books is extremely alarming. Women should not be forced to accept—and learn to cope with—men's bad behaviors. And the sad truth? These behaviors are merely symptoms of the underlying problems: 1) Men's lack of understanding and introspection concerning their actions (or inaction), and 2) women laboring under the damaging misconceptions of their childhood programming/ brainwashing regarding what being a woman is all about; and

NOTES

as a consequence, giving permission for these relationship-damaging behaviors, and oftentimes even condoning them.

The key to these kinds of changes is for both men and women to understand—and then do the slow, hard work to internalize—certain crucial techniques and behaviors. Men need to address their own flaws and stop asking the women in their lives to constantly adjust their thinking so as to accommodate men's bad behavior. The time has come for men to be accountable for their defects, to take positive action, and to alter their behavior in order to improve the quality of their relationships—and their lives. Here are a few examples of the concepts you will read about in the upcoming chapters of this book—concepts I believe to be of utmost importance to women who are ready to re-program themselves:

- Excise the words "My husband won't let me" from your vocabularies

- Reject the familiar "victim" role and take responsibility for your lives

- Gain insight into the world of men

- Learn about the difficulties that face the man who chooses to Evolve from a run-of-the-mill male, into an articulate, knowledgeable, charming, funny, thoughtful, and emotionally-available Evolved Man.

Women can reclaim their sanity and individuality, and men can improve their self-image and introduce stability and self-accountability to their relationships; marriages can be saved.

In the pages that follow, dear Reader, I will explain the Evolutionary path I have taken on my life-long journey to better myself and my outlook on life; a journey that rejects

NOTES

antiquated tenets of acceptable male behavior. My personal path is an inexorable pursuit of life—life lived comfortably in my own skin, as a complete *man*: loving and loved, funny yet intense, strong and sexually well-defined. I've learned to treasure the feminine characteristics I have allowed to awaken in myself; characteristics I've worked hard to integrate in my personality; normal feminine characteristics that reside in all men, but have been squashed because they're viewed as traditionally and *exclusively* female.

I have occasionally found my true brethren on the same path I embarked on, as we/they struggle with fears of the unknown… of abandoning the beaten path (read: being different)…fear of using untested guts that may have atrophied from lack of use. Very predictable and understandable fears, in the light of not having had any childhood role models who would have passed down a realistic moral compass to guide us. It is a path of principles and character, but one that clearly goes against the grain of society; an alternate life path for those choosing to enlighten themselves, and to raise their consciousness to a higher plane.

Ladies and Gentlemen, welcome to the world of the Evolved Man.

NOTES

Chapter 1:
The World of Men

What the hell is wrong with men today? Where are the **gentlemen**—brimming with class, dressing with style, walking with confidence, acting with integrity and honor, using proper tenses when they speak, and articulating their thoughts with finesse? Men who are hip and cool without the need to show their strength by intimidating and yelling at their children if they bring home a bad grade on their report card. Men who recognize that opening a door, or giving up a seat for a woman is simply *the right thing to do*, and not considered foreplay. Men who recognize that cursing can be offensive, but that used correctly (on occasion) can add emphasis to a statement. Are these men gone forever? Today's men seem to be more concerned with which teams are hitting the field this Sunday, than with the emotional welfare of the person they chose as their lifemate. (And I use the neutral word "lifemate" to point out that both homosexual and heterosexual couples struggle with the same kinds of relationship issues.)

Don't get me wrong. I have nothing against sports or any other traditionally masculine activity. I love playing a

NOTES

variety of sports, and I catch various sporting events on TV as my schedule allows. Good sportsmanship, teamwork, camaraderie, and a sense of fair play are great qualities—important qualities I hope both my son and daughter strive to incorporate as part of their lives. But I'm not referring to "male activities." I'm talking about the attitude of the stereotypic Man's Man toward the world.

Perhaps we should start with that term, "Man's Man." This term has always been used to describe certain men as being the embodiment of machismo, chutzpah, guts; fearlessness, aggression, relentless ambition; men who always keep a watchful eye on the prize, with nerve to spare. Over time, "Man's Man" has taken on an expanded definition to connote specific actions that call to mind an iconic, male-dominant visual: As the camera zooms in, we see the silhouette of a tall, slender man rising against a backdrop of an old western town; well-worn boots, jeans, a tattered hat, his rugged face and hands weathered by hard work; his eyes squinting from the sun. A dusty wind rolls across his spurs, and his vest rustles in the wind as he takes a long drag from his hand- rolled cigarette. In other words, society's version of the ultimate "Man's Man"—the Marlboro Man. (Notwithstanding society's stamp of approval, at least one of the Marlboro Man models was gay.)

Those bygone days and the barefoot-and-pregnant images they conjure up—as nostalgic and *Leave It To Beaver*-ish as they may be for some people—are long passed, and intelligent people on both sides of the gender equator know it. Not all women are the sweet and demure cookie-makers and boo-boo kissers of yesteryear. (read: "Dinner's on the table, dear, and the kids are in bed. How was your day? Do you need a shoulder massage?") There are countless smart, introspective, and goal-oriented women who are loving and emotionally available, and who *also* know what they want in their lives. The problems women have in their romantic relationships

NOTES

2

seem to boil down to one simple fact: In addition to having to constantly demand the respect and admiration they are due, many women are fed up with the constant barrage of shit they receive from the men in their lives.

Women have long lamented having to put up with difficult issues and habits. Up until the inception of the feminist movement, their complaints were perceived as anti-male soliloquies, and were ignored—and then quickly erased from the public consciousness of our male-skewed society. The real contradiction? A man's way of life causes him a multitude of problems that beg for—and would greatly benefit from—female intervention. But women are not "permitted" to complain; a no-win situation. Women have been forced to be understanding, accepting, and patient. To be, in a word, stoic. But how much can women endure? When will men *listen* as well as hear? When do we, as Evolved Men, acknowledge and accept not only that our houses need a "woman's touch", but that our primal instinct-driven souls are in desperate need of a swift kick in the ass?

The bad news is that a man and his lifestyle are not easily parted. Despite the reasoning, bitching, and sometimes outright hatred that come their way, men are always testing the limits of women's patience and tenacity; in fact, their very humanity…

> "The hamper is *right there*! If I find his underwear on the bathroom floor one more time, I'm gonna kill that son-of-a-bitch."

> "I don't need you to *solve* my problems. I need you to *listen* to me. Are you capable of just *listening*?"

> "Why do you think you know what I need? Have you ever *asked* me what I need?"

NOTES

Fortunately, nature has a way of providing some level of balance. Men have traditionally been the hunters/gatherers/protectors—usually performing well at primal tasks for their lifemate and family; so, it may be possible to overlook—or perhaps forgive—some of their deficiencies on a short-term basis. However, women suffer greatly from being forced to deal with core flaws that many men have for the whole of their lives. These defects not only negatively affect relationships/marriages over the long haul, but also *seriously impact the very success, confidence, and effectiveness of the men themselves.*

These flawed behavior patterns are all-too-familiar to me; I've had to deal with them first-hand, in my own personality—and grow past them. Moreover, as I gathered material for this book, I heard hundreds of men and women discussing these same behavioral difficulties in painstaking detail. I suppose the Cro-Magnon man's significant other could have perceived these behaviors as positive attributes under the right circumstances—perhaps. However, if we dare to call ourselves *civilized,* and call contemporary life a modern *civilization,* clearly these characteristics need to be put out to pasture. Let's examine these deficiencies one at a time.

Core Flaw #1: Über-dominance

Men know everything. We know how to drive, so just sit there and shut up. We know how to navigate perfectly, too, so stop pestering us to stop to ask for directions. (Sure, there have been plenty of jokes made about men's refusal to ask for directions when driving, but the comic quality is totally absent when one lives with that attitude, day in and day out.) We are the appointed/anointed remote control experts; just watch what we're watching. (And *please* be quiet! The game is on!) We are automatically great in bed, so just lay there; it'll feel good for both of us in a second or two. ("Um... sorry, Honey. I know that was fast. Gimmie a few minutes and we'll

NOTES

go again, okay?") We know what you need. We are the all-wise, all-knowing, all-seeing experts of the universe, and you are the bitch we bonked on the head and dragged back to our cave. We know *exactly* what you require: a father, a caretaker, a God that arbitrarily denies you your right to spend money (even if *you* are the breadwinner), your right to build your own life, and occasionally grants you permission to use your time for things you want to do— provided all your chores are done, the kids are in bed, and you've been a good girl.

If any of what you just read rings a bell, it is because many men have the overwhelming need to dominate… everything. We don't feel we're doing our jobs unless we mark our territory by figuratively peeing on everything within a 1,000-foot radius. And it's a damn shame, too. By intimidating and/or outright bullying, men often alienate the very people they are attempting to lead. An ancient, anonymous adage addressed the subject of leadership performed in this dominance-centric fashion… and its propensity for failure. To paraphrase:

> To lead effectively, vigilance and control of yourself and your surroundings is required. You must be out in front with your followers behind you. If your leadership techniques turn to dominance and you begin leading with coercion and oppression, you may look behind you and find that you are leading no one and only following yourself.

Some dominance is good, though… necessary, in fact. There is an inherent need in any healthy relationship for one person to be dominant; to be in power, so to speak. But power should not sit permanently with one person; it must be shared. A relationship needs a bit of push/pull to be successful. Alpha personalities take the lead, but male Alphas need to learn that intermittently passing the "baton of power" is vital to the survival of a healthy relationship.

NOTES

The concept I've been kind of circling around is simple: control. Control and command of all things in their domain is the gauge by which men measure themselves, and each other. To see this in action, let's virtually observe a group of five men on a Friday night. In this hypothetical group, four men are single, and one has a wife or girlfriend. One of the single men asks, "You going out with us tonight?" The romantically-involved man has a choice to make when answering. If he gives an honest answer (which more than likely is that his better half does not want him drinking and clubbing with a group of potentially morally-challenged miscreants), he is dubbed "whipped." So, in all likelihood, he lies: "Naw, man, I just feel like kickin' back at home tonight." Bullshit. If he were really in control of his life and felt confident about the life path he was on, he would tell his friends the truth, regardless of what they would think. And that, dear Reader, is *real* control; true rule over one's self, and the confidence to show it.

Dominance and control are concepts men worship in every facet of their lives. We thrill at it in every boxing match we watch, and every car we pass on the freeway. Being "in charge" of a woman is an extension of our need to control everything in our lives. It is carefully instilled in us from a very young age ("Watch your sister and keep her out of trouble!") and it stays with us. It is dominance that allows men to see themselves as strong, courageous, and brave. The flip side of that positive self-perception, unfortunately, is arrogance. It is the misuse of dominance that upsets the natural order of civilized, Evolved relationships... and it's that misuse that young boys see in their parents' relationships that is the catalyst for boys to learn to build their own masculine self-image *on the wrong things.*

Perhaps the process that really moves the male-dominance meter is the building of a career. Let's look at a

NOTES

6

common scenario: A man finishes his schooling, and begins a career in business. He makes the arduous climb up the proverbial corporate ladder, and through hard work (with just a pinch of luck) he becomes successful. Success brings supervisory duties, raises, and affluence. At this point, many men embrace their careers, but keep a careful balance of home life and work life—leaving the office at the office, and being mentally present when at home. However, for some men there is a fundamental shift in their behavior, and one of two things happens: 1) He internalizes the new feelings of self-worth and respect from people at his job, and interprets them as: Through hard work comes reward, and that reward is power. Or, 2) He brings his newfound power home, and rules the roost (or attempts to) the way he "rules" at his job. Sorry, gents. In today's civilized culture, this just isn't how it works.

The only way for men to grow beyond an insatiable desire for control is to view the need to always dominate as one does a bad habit, like smoking. Quitting takes awareness, perseverance, willpower, and most of all, a willingness to *want* to rein in one's need to control. *In order to stop power struggles, men need to listen more than they speak, accept more than they criticize, and believe more than they doubt when they relate to the women in their lives.* For this concept to take firm hold and alter behavior, men at the beginning of their Evolution need... training. (Much more on this later.)

Core Flaw #2: Etiquette (or lack thereof)

Manners and gentlemanly conduct should be synonymous, but many of my brothers have missed this boat. Releasing a 15-second three-octave fart (in mixed company!)—one so foul it makes the dog leave the room—seems to be a standing goal with men of all ages, 9 to 90 (although I do not know

NOTES

how you would put that skill on a résumé). Men have discovered that a human being's normal bodily functions can cover a multitude of offensive behaviors, and they compete for bragging rights across a wide range of "events": gas (both ends), picking, chewing, scratching, adjusting, rubbing, and a seemingly endless concentration on volume (measured in both decibels and quantity). I wish I could understand why these activities trigger feelings of bonding for men, not to mention the jargon that accompanies these behaviors: the Dutch Oven (passing gas in bed and then suffocating your mate by pulling the covers over her head), the Dismount (action taken after a very loud belch or rear-end emission, resembling a gymnastics pose struck after finishing a routine), a Soprano (a man who passes gas with a sound that is high-pitched; also known as a Squeaker), ad nauseum. Take note, men: These habits are disgusting, offensive, and are not considered endearing to the women in your lives. Keys are not Q-Tips®, nails should be clipped in private, whisker trimmings should be wiped off the sink, privates can be adjusted—as well as gas passed—in the lavatory, and ripped underwear and holey socks should be thrown away and replaced.

Throughout the 17+ years I have known my wife (to include the time when we first began dating), I have yet to practice these repulsive behaviors in front of her or our kids. What happens in our sleep is not our fault; it comes with being a human being. But a conscious effort needs to be put forth to not to engage in these activities when one is around other people (uh, duh?). It's really just basic civility. Men who systematically shun civilized behavior and imagine obnoxious behavior to be "a guy thing" or "what guys do," are perverting *true* masculinity. Moreover, men seem to assume that these offensive activities are automatically acceptable in the company of other men—whether they're with men they've known for some time, or are with those they've just met.

NOTES

8

Personal Account:

About 10 years ago, I met with a reporter from the Wall Street Journal for lunch at *The Slanted Door*, a popular restaurant in San Francisco. As a marketing executive, I was there to pitch him on my company's services, and was looking for editorial coverage and possibly an interview for my then-CEO. After we were seated in a quiet section of the restaurant, we exchanged pleasantries, and quickly reviewed the menu. And then the unimaginable occurred. The reporter smiled, raised his leg, and passed gas (and **not** quietly). I was shocked. I suppose he felt it was acceptable as we were in an isolated section of the restaurant, and… we are both men. However, I couldn't get past it. Without a word, I rose from my seat and left. Obviously I wasn't able to secure the editorial mention we were looking for at that time. However, my sense of etiquette cannot be compromised. Disgusting is disgusting. Period.

'Nuff said. Moving on…

A man's actions that are gallant, respectful, brave, and courteous are regarded as extensions of etiquette: chivalry. Let's consider the etymology of that word for a moment. *Chivalry* comes from the Middle English *chivalrie,* taken from the French word *chevalier,* or knight. The references to shining armor, swordplay, and the Round Table are common knowledge.

> Chivalry—Civility or polite attention, especially to ladies. Nobility of spirit or action; courage; courtliness.

NOTES

The word "gallantry" is synonymous with chivalrous actions, and digging a little deeper reveals an interesting, lesser-known definition of "gallant":

> *Attention or courtesy designed to win sexual favors from a female.*

Even back in medieval times, men had it down cold. Treat 'em right, even if you have to lie, and you'll have her in bed in no time.

The typical man behaves in a chivalrous manner (modern definition) with three types of women, listed here in order of priority: his mother; women he is currently sleeping with; and women he wants to sleep with—or would sleep with, given the opportunity.

About Mothers: His mother comes first—often before his wife, which can be a separate problem in itself. Experts debate the many deep-rooted, Freudian reasons for this—the man's childhood environment, whether or not he was breastfed, his family's social standing, and many other factors may play a part—all of which are out of my area of expertise. We may not know the "why" of it, but couples live that problem in their relationships, nevertheless.

About Sexual Prospects: These types of women are not as clear-cut, because they're based on a man's mental state at specific points in time. Let us assume, for a moment, that he is honoring the vows of fidelity he and his wife made to each other. **But,** if that buxom blonde on the train during his morning commute coyly glances his way with the corners of her mouth turned up, it's a good bet that he will give up his seat. The attraction is there, so he acts. On the flip side: If the attraction is not there for him, it's not that he refuses to act; He's **completely unaware** that there is an opportunity to act at all.

NOTES

It has been painful to observe men in many situations when they show brazen disregard for the women they don't/wouldn't want to sleep with; painful, and in an odd way it's almost fascinating. Much of the behavior I have observed defies understanding. To wit: Older men opening a door for a young woman who appears to be around 22, and then letting that door in the face of an attractive 50-something woman who was walking directly behind her.

I've seen many men speaking intently to the breasts of a woman—as if her nipples were ears—while ignoring the woman standing nearby who simply needs him to move out of the way so she can pass; and on and on…

Men who choose to notice opportunities to treat women with respect and courtesy—instead of like sexual marks—will find a never-ending storehouse of possibilities by merely opening their eyes in everyday life. It takes very little effort, and makes everyone feel good. The ability to put a smile on a woman's face, make her laugh, or have her look at you appreciatively is an incredible feeling, albeit one that most men truly experience only a few times in their lives. It doesn't matter if you (or they) are married. Acting chivalrous is non-sexual in nature. Modern-day chivalry is more than action. It is a state of mind where men are honorable and courteous to all *people*—that is, *men as well as women.* (Warning! Homophobic men, please stop reading *immediately*!) Yes, men like to be "charmed" by other men, and for the same reasons women do: It is a feeling of being cared about, and in some ways, loved… as a *person*. It bears repeating: **These behaviors have nothing to do with sex-based motivations.** They are borne of one's emotions, though, and I suppose could be incorrectly grouped with the New Age nonsense-term "male bonding." I realize that "male bonding" and the images this media-coined expression conjures up are bad for the eyes and ears. Let me be clear: I'm not talking about cuddling parties, or the like. I *am* talking about caring, conversation,

NOTES

wit, and courtesy. These are the same men who always seem to have a group around them at a party; talking, laughing, and entertaining. Men who are clever, witty, smooth, and cool (with just a touch of boldness) do attract people of both genders. Women want them, and men want to be like them (or at a minimum, be associated with them).

A man's chivalry toward other men also includes elements of awareness and genuine interest.

Personal Account:
A number of years ago while walking on a street in downtown San Francisco, I noticed a construction crew working feverishly on a large building project—a formidable undertaking. One of the workers was near the fence line, and I inquired as to how long the crew had been working on the job. After he answered, I said, "Wow, it looks great. You guys are real pros. You must be very proud." After a few seconds, his face changed a little bit, and as I took my cue to continue on my way, he overcame his hesitation and said, "Hey, thanks! This is nothing. You should see the last job we worked on." We then spoke for about an hour, and I found that I wasn't talking with the oft-maligned stereotypic catcaller/member of a construction crew.

So, why did he respond and speak with me so candidly, instead of passing me off as a nut? I followed up with him a few weeks later to find out why, and he told me many interesting thoughts. In essence, he said I had reached him in a way he hadn't experienced before, and that he'd never considered his job a real source of pride

NOTES

until that moment. He thought it incredible that some stranger—let alone a man—was sincerely impressed with his work. He went on to explain to me that the day he and I had first met, he'd mentioned our meeting to his wife. Evidently she was not surprised by my comments, and took the opportunity to tell him that she had been proud of him for years. In short, my chivalrous actions caused him to open up, which in turn strengthened his bond with his wife; and it all had to do with how he *felt* when I took a moment to sincerely reach out to him *as a person*, and to acknowledge his work. It was simple, sincere, and changed his outlook on himself and his marriage.

I offer the above example from my life to reiterate that chivalry is **not** exclusive to romance-incited actions. Modern-day chivalry is about affecting *people* and the way they *feel about themselves*, and its effects are far-reaching and long-lasting. When a man pulls out a chair for a woman, it isn't what he did that impressed her (although she *thinks* it is). For that moment in time, she feels that she *matters*, like the world revolves around her. It is *that* feeling that makes the difference—for men as well as for women.

Core Flaw #3: Infidelity

Where is it written that men must scatter their seed in as many fields as possible? To answer this question, let us reflect on one stage of development in male adolescence I'll casually refer to as the "Young, Dumb, Full-of-Cum" phase. (Crass? Yes. Accurate? Definitely.)

During most of my teens and early twenties, I ran amuck with a group of six other guys. We were inseparable... the

NOTES

quintessential best-of-friends—crazy, funny, charming, and I daresay, good-looking (or at least that was what we were told). For purposes of fleshing out this anecdote so you can see how some parts of my youth were lived, I'll combine those elements with: 1) a constantly throbbing hard-on; 2) a total of 18 years of experience on the planet; 3) a cool car, popularity, and a bit of cash in our pockets. It should be readily apparent that this is *not* a recipe for establishing relationships built on fidelity.

All would not be lost, though. With age comes experience. Therefore, it's logical for us to expect that upon growing physically and mentally, this group of horny teenagers should have "sown their wild oats" (read: gotten it out of their systems—if you'll pardon the pun), and matured into upstanding men of their communities who lead, love, and live using their brains, not their privates. The fundamental elements so glaringly absent from the minds and lives of many teenagers (a sense of ethics, a realistic understanding of the concept of "cause and effect" of one's actions) are behaviors and beliefs we expect to find well integrated in the lives of adult men. Right? Well... unfortunately that isn't reality in today's multi-partner world.

Many of my old friends—today, almost all from that time are *former* friends—are still living through their teenage shadows, and their wives (second wives, in most cases) are paying for it. It appears that the main challenge is to cheat and not get caught. (Or... perhaps getting caught *is* the goal. That's how they can leave their wives and "live the life she stole from me" without having to actually be the one to directly make that decision. Men like this are (forgive me, but I must call it as I see it) without courage, and evidently incapable of communicating directly—not only with the woman in their lives, but with most of the people with whom they interact. You may be thinking that this example is peculiar to just my life; it's not. Nor is it embellished. Through the extensive

NOTES

interviewing of both men and women (as well as going back to talk to people who were still connected to my former friends, in order to get the real dirt... *shhh!*), I have found that the sorry state of affairs (again, no pun intended) I've just described is not unique. It is just one example to show how the misguided behaviors of many young men become the standard operating mode of today's stereotypic man.

Society has always quietly condoned men behaving like "studs" while remaining "happily married." This oxymoronical viewpoint is apparently spoken from the same side of the mouth that says a woman who sleeps with—or even just pursues—multiple partners is a slut, a whore, and a tramp. Obviously, men concoct these views; men that, if they had their way, would have women lie down as whores— catering to their every sexual whim—and rise in their post-coital afterglow as virgins.

This kind of widespread dogma, seemingly ingrained in one of the frontal lobes of society, is a trap; a trap that keeps men emotionally stunted, preventing so many of them from achieving the greatness they were meant to realize. It also keeps women meandering through life with no clear concept of their own self-esteem and power. The truly sad thing is that boys and girls are inculcated with these views from early childhood.

> *Personal Account:*
> While in high school, I read a study concerning parenting techniques and the effects of verbal reinforcement on young children. The name of the study has been lost to time, but I will never forget the details. The study was performed during the '60s. Fifty sets of parents and their children (50% boys, 50% girls) were placed in a private room and observed for 60 minutes through one-way

NOTES

glass. Creative materials were placed in the room for the children to play with—blocks, crayons, pens and paper. All of the children created some type of project, (e.g., a tower of blocks, a drawing, etc.) They then brought the finished projects to their parents. Of the 25 sets of parents with sons, 24 responded by telling the child, "Good job!" In contrast, all 25 sets of parents with daughters responded by saying, "Good girl!" The subliminal message was clear to me: When you perform a task as a man, you earn recognition, pride, self-satisfaction, and the feeling of reward that comes from the acknowledgement of a job well done. The girls performing the same task were taught something very different: Accomplishing a task was not something that promoted pride, but instead defined them as acceptable.

As we grow to adulthood with these views, men aren't the only people affected. A woman's self-view is significantly influenced, and as a consequence, skewed... becoming quite evident if she establishes a pattern of being in emotionally stunting, damaging relationships. Think about this: There are many men who are successful, and their successes are chalked up to the man's drive, talent, skill luck, or a combination of some, or all of those elements. But there's a glaring omission: There are *so many* men who are successful *specifically because they have the right women in their lives*—their girlfriend, or their wife, or their mother, or their sister—*who handle 99% of everything in their day-to-day living.* This allows the man to be able to concentrate on only one single thing—his success. A truism: "Behind every great man is a woman." I would argue that perhaps, "In front of every potentially great woman is an underdeveloped, mediocre man who won't get out of her way." But I digress...

NOTES

16

Sexual conquests in a man's life can cross over into a previously unmentioned area where modern-day chivalry does not exist; a place where women claim chivalry is dead. Many women have a lack of self-assurance so pronounced, that they end up settling for relationships that are void of intimacy, romance, and the closeness that comes when sharing one's self with another person; relationships that are completely devoid of the normal emotional vulnerability that grows out of shared feelings of trust. But there are reasons women end up in this predicament. Let's look at the process: He did the initial work, and craftily coerced you into bed. Now that he's had you, there is no reason for him to go that extra mile… unless, of course, he wants you sexually again. (That's part of the reason we have flower shops strategically located at airports, shopping malls, and within a stone's throw of friendly neighborhood bars.) Married or single, these women are meant to wait, and to feel grateful that he even allowed them to sleep with him in the first place; wait… and wait… until their services are again required.

> "Men are on their best behavior at the beginning of a courtship, but things start to slip as they become more comfortable in the relationship."
> —*Countless women in unhappy relationships*

Unmarried men usually start to relax a short time into a new relationship, and begin to show their un-Evolved nature. Married men call it "getting comfortable"—a behavior no Evolved man exhibits.

I can relate to these situations, as I've been on both sides; both as a "comfortable man dating" and as an Evolved man. I candidly disclosed earlier in this book that I originally matriculated from the University of Life with a major in Womanizer, and a minor in Insensitivity To Others. I raised a lot of hell growing up, had numerous sexual partners

NOTES

(some of whom I don't remember, some of whom I *sincerely* hope don't remember me), and was a general cad. In all its malignancy, this promiscuous phase of life was rendered benign as I became involved in a serious relationship with the woman who was to become my wife. Once we began courting and it became clear to me that this was indeed the real thing, I was immediately hyper-thrust into growth and maturity. I *knew* I needed to give up shooting myself in the foot, and to begin expanding my working knowledge of love, honesty and intimacy... the path Evolved men find themselves on as they continue their growth.

Core Flaw #4: Emotional Availability

It must be confusing to women as to why men don't openly relate to each other with any real emotion. It has certainly been confusing to me. Most men gloss over the seriousness or depth of their relationships, and use common defense mechanisms of various sorts—humor, denial, and anger. These ways of having superficial arm's-length relationships with male friends also bleed into their romantic relationships, and women experience the distance as the emotional disconnection it is. The typical example:

> Woman: "Honey, we never talk anymore. Let's just sit and talk tonight."
>
> Man: "We never talk? We're talking right now."

The "conversation" could then take a turn for the worse, and the couple finds themselves discussing/arguing about how they don't converse anymore, instead of *just talking and relating.* Or, perhaps he'll brusquely say something that totally shuts down any possibility of a pleasant verbal exchange, like, "Let me just relax, Hon... I've had a long week."

NOTES

18

Why are men emotionally unavailable? The simple fact is that (as a general statement) most men don't know how to get close and *stay* close to anyone… not even to themselves. It's probable that this is due to primal instincts—from thousands of years ago—that enabled men to get into a relationship in order to ensure the survival of the species, and stay in it for a certain amount of time—perhaps for as long as it took to prepare their children to take care of themselves, to make them ready to fly the coop, so to speak.

A Man's Man really doesn't know how to "connect" with himself, let alone with the woman in his life. So, would he connect with other *men*? Please. In American culture, anything beyond a handshake or a hearty slap on the back is viewed as potential evidence of homosexuality; with the exception, of course, of the society-approved touching while playing sports. During athletic events, ass-patting is a commonly-accepted gesture among macho jocks. Dr. Freud would have had a field day with that one. I won't even get into the whole subject of wrestling.

The simple truth is that many men aren't comfortable in their own skin. They are afraid to see things from an emotional point of view. Instead, men play it off as the woman's fault, claiming that the women in their lives are too: needy, clingy, demanding, bitchy, bossy, annoying, emotional… and the ubiquitous charge of being "over-sensitive". But in truth, it's the discomfort a man has with *himself* that causes emotional distance. He is *afraid to lose control* and only be *equal* in the relationship. Being just equal in the relationship feels to him like a giant step down. In summary, men are *very* insecure. They would never admit that, but it's completely accurate, nonetheless.

Insecurity is the culprit, and it's at the root of most of the bad behaviors and habits of a Man's Man, to include the core flaws I have outlined in this chapter. Insecurity is the reason he often thinks the woman in his life is cheating, the

NOTES

reason he speaks loudly even when she's standing right next to him, and the reason he's constantly worried about virility and penis size. Men need to be perceived as omnipotent, and they refuse to show what they believe to be weaknesses.

> *She says: "Need directions?"*
> "Got it covered. I have a great sense of direction, so we won't need a map."
>
> *She tells him she has a problem at her job:*
> "Problem at your job? I know how to solve it. Here's what you do…"
>
> *Need a shoulder to cry on?*
> "Here I am… but don't cry forever. We need to fix this problem, and I can help."
>
> *She tells him "Put yourself in **my** shoes for a minute. Look at this through **my** eyes—not through yours—and then tell me what you feel."*
> "Huh?"

The above examples—even though a couple of them are rooted in best intentions—illustrate a disturbing emotional defect of today's Man's Man: They can be there in time of *solvable* need… but if asked to put themselves in another's shoes, or to identify with where another person is at, emotionally (otherwise known as being capable of *empathy),* men become lost and simply don't know what to do, or how to behave. It's not a tangible request, and so a man doesn't have any idea as to how to dig into his *self* and just identify, acknowledge, *feel, empathize;* not solve.

It is insecurity and emotional unavailability that keep men from fully engaging their significant others. It would seem that men find it easier to keep emotional distance—in

NOTES

the interest of "self preservation"—thereby risking the loss of someone they hold dear. Interestingly, many men *will* risk the fall into intimacy later in life, as they tend to become more emotionally available as they age.

To conclude, dear Reader, the world of men is a noisy, testosterone-laden swirling vortex of bullshit. Men seem to mainly operate from what I view as their natural "talent" of being passive-aggressive. I'm of the opinion that they appear to almost enjoy wallowing in mediocrity, as they sit comfortably in boxers amidst yesterday's dirty dishes; performing only the minimum they think is required to keep women from complaining, and engaging in just enough foreplay to provide lubrication. If men could break out of this caveman mentality and see what kind of human beings they truly are—and see the perception women have of them—it would be blindingly obvious to them why divorce rates are up, kids' grades are down, and why the women they claim to love are taking enough anti-depressants to put even Keith Richards into a drunken stupor.

NOTES

Chapter II:
Women and The World of Men

And now, a word from the other side. I've bashed my Brothers; much of the truth is now out. But what does it mean? Let's put it in context. (Sorry, guys, they deserve this information. We've held our secrets long enough; time to level the playing field.)

Men get away with murder with the women in their lives. They do pretty much what they want, say what they want, and keep the women in their lives down (intentionally or unintentionally). And why? Part of the fault lies with women who allow men to misbehave in their relationships, but there's much more to this problem. Men controlling/manipulating women is accepted by society, and is in many ways encouraged. A large percentage of women have a compulsive need to fix, change and/or save the men who are in their lives. In contrast, many men have an overwhelming need to cheat, ignore, lie (by omission or by telling half-truths), and to take women for granted—the very women who are their life partners, women they've promised to honor and cherish. And how does this behavior affect women? They complain, criticize, bitch, and protest. But more often than

NOTES

not, these same women **do not follow through**, and men know it. Women accept the bad things in a relationship for a variety of supposedly justifiable reasons:

"I'm staying for the kids."

"But, I love him."

"He's such a good father."

"My man's not so bad compared to the others I've seen."

"I'm too old to play the field again."

"These are just rough spots in the marriage. I'll stick it out." *(Author's note: Ten years is not defined as a "rough spot"; it's called a way of life.)*

These are the precise fears and rationalizations that incapacitate thousands of women who—from childhood on—have been brainwashed by society. As adults, they take in emotional damage on a daily basis from the male figures they trust most. If one were a fly on the wall in many of today's homes, we would hear husbands giving endless negative messages: "Where would you go? What would you do?" And to the women who didn't prepare careers before they married: "You have no skills. You can't make it without me." Specious logic. And for the women who *did* prepare careers before walking down the aisle, a different set of challenges awaits.

Linda R. Hirshman wrote a very interesting book aptly titled *"Get To Work: A Manifesto For The Women Of The World"* (2006, Viking Adult). She brings to light many of the same issues I heard from the participants in my study. A key message from Ms. Hirshman's book resonated with me: A great percentage of women were found to have given up— or were in the process of giving up—their career aspirations (or established careers, in many cases) in order to stay at

NOTES

home to start a family. However, *they never returned to the workforce.*

The choice of having a career or being a stay-at-home mother is a very personal one. In certain ways, the latter is much more challenging than any career could be. I have the utmost respect for the stay-at-home moms of the world, and because I'm a man I would never pretend to know all the emotions and thoughts that going into making that decision. However, in many of these situations—and in line with Ms. Hirshman's views and research—I observed some striking similarities. By choosing—or by allowing their husbands to make the choice for them—to permanently give up their careers they are giving up their *independence and individuality,* and placing themselves in the position of being completely dependent on the man in their lives. Many of them had held positions of influence—lawyers, doctors, executives—and left their careers permanently for motherhood. These women are robbing society of their talents; talents sorely needed in today's testosterone-filled arenas, such as politics, healthcare, high-tech, the service industry, etc.

Many of the husbands seemed comfortable with that shift in power/control, believing that it is a man's job to provide and a woman's job to... well... do everything else. As I see the dynamics in these relationships, these women were forced/manipulated into giving up their *selves* in order to placate the man in their lives. Their husbands refused to regard their partners as equals—as people who have their own dreams, plans, and goals in addition to filling a chosen role of wife or mother.

On the flip side, there are many couples where the woman is a full-time mother *and* holds down a full-time career. In many of these kinds of situations, it strains the relationship to the breaking point. Take Melissa, a participant in my study, and a top executive at an advertising

NOTES

firm in New York. When she met Bryan—the man who would become her husband—they were both in middle management earning roughly the same salaries; he at his job, and she at hers. However, through a lot of effort and natural talent, Melissa's career hit its stride. After several years of working 60+-hour weeks, she broke through the Glass Ceiling and became a highly respected and well-paid senior executive. Taking over the firm as president was then a very real possibility on the horizon. But as her status, influence, and paycheck grew, her marriage began to deteriorate. She attempted to work on their relationship, but Bryan seemed to become uninterested, citing trivial issues as his reasons for his discontent. In addition to having to pick up the slack because of Melissa's long work hours—something many women must do by default—Bryan was genuinely threatened by her rapid advancement and success. After a year in marriage counseling, they divorced. Bryan, like so many other men, had his masculinity built on all the wrong things. His fragile ego couldn't handle that she was building something for herself—in this case, a solid career. Before their split, Melissa and Bryan had terrible fights—the vast majority of which were based on control. Even though she was the major wage earner, Bryan had grown very passive-aggressive, creating problems and roadblocks for Melissa. As a result, she was forced to manage the house, in addition to holding down her demanding job. Returning from work each day, she had to transport their 12 and 14-year-old daughters to after-school activities, then monitor their homework, and take over the shopping, finance management; everything. The real issue here, obviously, is Bryan's lack of respect and emotional support for Melissa… which we know stems from his own insecurities.

This problem—a Man's Man dealing in an extremely poor manner with having a wife who earns money—is a multi-faceted subject itself, and it points up one of the grave difficulties most men have in Evolving to a higher level of

NOTES

consciousness. Let's take a look at how the whole house of cards comes down—if couples have even been struggling to learn how to build one up: It has become quite clear that the whole concept of masculinity dictated by society is largely based on all the wrong things. It's just one gigantic—and shameful—set-up. Boys learn very early in their lives that to be a "real man," they must be the major (if not the sole) breadwinners. And therein lies the set-up: For the poor and middle class in this society, (as well as in the societies of many other countries), this type of plan has not been economically feasible for quite some time, as making ends meet requires two salaries. And when we mix in other profound societal issues, the problems grow exponentially. The male/female equality issue, for one—which in itself has many sub-issues (e.g., equality in committed relationships, equal time/effort investment in maintaining the house and the children who live in it, the whole Pandora's Box of equal opportunity/equal pay for women in the workplace…glass ceilings, etc.)— and we dare not fail to address an enormous health problem affecting men, that also affects the women and children in their lives. I'm talking about the plethora of men who have bought into the myth of what a man's role in life should be as "the provider"… which leads us to the staggering realization that society is now facing an astronomical increase in stress-induced heart disease.

The Man's Man personality construct wreaks havoc in every situation he's in. To wit:

I found a large segment of society in which a married "Man's Man" refers to his spouse as "the wife," as in "the car" or "the dog." Uh… hello? Isn't the phrase "my old lady" a statement of yesteryear? Evidently not. References like these may start as affectionate pet names, but over time they quietly undermine the equality in a relationship, desensitizing a woman and preparing her for more and more demeaning behavior. Before you know it, a woman is having

NOTES

27

a conversation like the one Marie in Houston had with her best friend:

> "You have such beautiful hair, Marie, but it would look <u>really</u> gorgeous with some blonde highlights. Why don't you get it done?"
>
> "I can't. My husband would never let me."

"Let me?" Huh? At twenty-seven years old, three-and-a-half years of marriage, college degree, 16-month-old son, Marie found herself completely under her husband's thumb—by choice. During our interview, I reminded her that it was *her body*, and that it was a personal decision to do *anything* she chose to it: tattoos, ear piercing, hairstyle, or whatever. I added that friends and spouses listen to each other, and in the event of disagreement, can find a compromise... but at its core, this was a decision about her... her personal wants. She listened, but was unsure. Apparently, brainwashing takes very little time, and her friend was completely taken aback—as was I! I mean, it's *her hair!* Marie's husband apparently believes that it's his **right** (read: within the realm of being a man) to grant or deny permission for his spouse on a case-by-case basis. And Marie apparently had the same belief. It's important to note that the *real* person in control here was Marie, as she made the decision to *give up*. By doing so, she enabled someone else to dictate and control her, *but it was a choice*.

These issues—taught in childhood and reinforced all the way to adult life—have bolstered society's sense of masculinity. I want to re-state something loudly and clearly; something that women—and more importantly, men—need to hear repeatedly: Today's Man's Man is building his character and his relationships on a defective foundation, guaranteed to crumble. Men are seemingly quite comfortable with the way things are, but when you strip away the façade of pleasantness, many women are unhappy with the way

NOTES

their relationships are progressing (or not progressing, in many cases). To rectify this, women need to make some fundamental changes in how they relate to the man in their lives, and move beyond only feeling worthwhile when there are "praised."

Wake up! Stop being a victim!

In my younger/pre-Evolution days, my cohorts and I would subconsciously seek out women that were not dedicated to their own self-worth… then we would control and dominate the relationship. But let me be clear: We were not abusers. I suppose we could be most aptly described as opportunistic conmen. (A conman is different than a hustler. Hustlers get what they came for and vacate the premises immediately. Conmen have the uncanny ability to stay likeable—even lovable—and thus can stay around until they *choose* to leave.) We said and did what was necessary to achieve our goals (which, more often than not, were to simply get laid,). Obviously, these weren't genuine "relationships," but it was a dance that all parties chose to play—we, as the miscreants, and the ladies as our… well… victims. For a time, the women we were involved with felt special. We told them what they wanted to hear, and did what it took to get what we wanted. Once we got it, we were able to provide a myriad of excuses/ explanations of why we were: busy, unavailable, unable to hear the phone, keeping the living room curtains closed 24/7, angry, out at 3 a.m. without calling, out of cell phone battery power, or out with a female "friend" who she'd never met. ("But Babe, she's a old friend from school. She's here on business and I wanted to catch up.") And what did the women do after being faced with this obviously questionable behavior and our subsequent bullshit excuses? They were very upset (and rightfully so), but most of them wouldn't sever the relationships. It was as though the good times were worth the blatant miscommunications, lies, deceits, drama, and general bullshit. (And, let me take this opportunity to

NOTES

acknowledge all the pain I caused them. You didn't deserve it, and you are owed an apology. Ladies—you know who you are—please know that I'm deeply sorry for all that shit. You were—unfortunately—part of my growth into an Evolved Man.)

But back to my pre-Evolution days. The women my friends and I dated—like so many of the women I spoke with—were clear as to "their place" in the relationship hierarchy: demure, submissive, controlled. Even if their submissive feelings were only subconscious, they acted as if they *wanted* to be treated badly... like they somehow deserved it. It's not that we went out of our way to treat them poorly, but the dynamics were perfect: They were looking for a man who was unattainable, and who would say and do the right things for them—even if it were only on a temporary basis—and we were ready to provide the minimum to get what we wanted. Interest in this type of man may derive from a variety of places, but the issues described here are merely symptoms... and we are again circling around Core Flaw #1: Control.

Men are at the root of these issues, but they're not entirely at fault. Women allow—and consistently invite—men to treat them like emotional punching bags. This cycle needs to be stopped... but women need to apply the brakes. They need to stop playing Jesus to their man's Pontius Pilate. Women deserve much more, and can avoid these damaging relationship issues by demanding more, and sticking to their guns.

The most common comment I heard from nearly every woman approaching the end of a relationship is that "something was missing." But through discussion, they discovered that what was missing wasn't something from the relationship; it was missing from **their** life. As we spoke together, a number of women discovered what that "something" was: a sense of *self-accomplishment,* coupled with their partner being supportive and proud of what they were

NOTES

building *as women, not as wives or mothers.* These women—like so many others—had taken some significant hits to their self-esteem from their husbands, boyfriends, fathers.... and from themselves. The advice I offered was this: Marriage is the biggest promise you can make to another person. But in order to (potentially) save their relationships, they needed to save *themselves.* Men either aren't aware or aren't interested in stopping this cycle, as they unconsciously or consciously think they have too much to lose—mainly, control. So, what is a forward-thinking, intelligent woman to do?

The Self-Esteem Dance of Death

If there is one major contributor to destructive relationships, it's lack of self-esteem. A Man's Man will lovingly feed a woman's ego until he realizes that providing and withdrawing love, attention and emotional support can be effective weapons; triggers that give him control. And that's when the destructive pattern begins. She wants his love and support (and rightly so), but she waits for it. He knows she's waiting, and keeps her on a string until the last possible second—then gives her the attention and love she so desires in order to placate her. Once she is satisfied he stops again, leaving her waiting... and round and round we go. Intermittent gratification... powerful stuff.

These self-esteem issues play a fundamental role in what women allow men to get away with in relationships. The majority of the participants were adamantly in agreement that their partner had changed and become much different than when they had first met them. Sally from New York:

> "Joe used to really love me. I used to get love letters, flowers. Now, it's like I'm just there to fuck him at his leisure... and even that's predictable—a blowjob, followed by the same 10 minutes of boring sex. Where's

NOTES

my attention? If I ask for it, it's not the same as if he gives it freely. After five years, he should know what the hell I want, if he paid attention."

In probing further, Sally and I discovered that the root issues of her dissatisfaction—lack of attention, lack of dedication, a feeling of being taken advantage of—were present long before they were married, which meant one of two possibilities had been at work: she didn't see the signs, or she ignored the signs. The true answer (that she ignored the signs) emerged as we kept looking at her situation and she had removed the rose-colored glasses. Comments like hers prove an old maxim: Women marry men thinking they will change, and they don't. Men marry women thinking they won't change, and they do.

Women faced with these issues have to make a conscious decision regarding the survival of their self-esteem and happiness. They will usually be choosing one of three paths: They can accept things the way they are, that their significant other most likely will not change. Or, they can fight head-to-head for the equality they deserve, and their needs to be filled. Or, they can work on becoming very introspective, and then work out a plan of action—**their own actions**—and stop looking for a relationship to solve their problems. In my opinion, the first two choices often fail. Blanket acceptance or fighting lead to resentment, and resentment can potentially lead to internal issues (emotional shut down, depression, sickness, rage) or external issues (destructive behavior, paranoia, murder). Women looking to better themselves and eliminate the problems in their marriage must change their tactics, just as men do on the battlefield in time of war. If a woman keeps pounding away from one certain position—arguing with her partner over an issue they have fought about many times, and in the

NOTES

exact same way she has always fought and never had gotten anywhere—it will be familiar to the man, and he will be completely prepared. Women must alter their approach and stay focused on the end goal—winning the war—instead of on winning immediate short-term battles. In *The Art of War*, Sun Tzu offers the following: "He will win who, prepared himself, waits to take the enemy unprepared." (That quote would read equally well, "She will win...")

The Three Elements of Transition

At the beginning of my journey of self-discovery, I learned that I needed to really ponder three fundamental questions until I had the answers to them; answers that would be uniquely mine. The answers to these questions would be unique to each person, and could be very helpful for finding a successful path in life. Here they are, listed in order of priority:

- Who am I?

- Where am I going?

- Who should accompany me on this journey through life?

These ideas, when considered and thought about, as opposed to just reading the words—were important points to get straight in my head when I made the transition from being a Man's Man to being an Evolved Man. And the same holds true for women: know yourself, know the direction you are headed, and know who you will choose to accompany you. If you marry prior to your own self-discovery, you may be setting yourself up for disappointment and failure.

Women: Do you know who you are and where you're going? Are you doing what you planned to do back when you were a kid, or have you spent most of the past years

NOTES

only raising kids? What is stopping you from achieving your greatness? Put your foot down and stop coasting through life... live *your* life. Having children doesn't preclude following your dreams and having goals. Demand the support and friendship you want and deserve from your lifemate. If he is real and true to himself—and to you—he will step up to the plate and help you achieve your goals. If no one else has told you, let me be the one who does: Regardless of who makes the money, who does the housework, who stays home with the kids, or who washes the car, you are not his mother; you are not his bitch; you are not a slave.

Men: When was the last time you asked her what *she* wanted out of life? Not your lives together; **her life, her goals, her dreams**—apart from kids, husband, and responsibilities. Have you ever asked her? If you haven't, it's time to take a hard look at why you haven't, and why you consciously or subconsciously don't want your mate to achieve her goals. Is she just there to do laundry and provide sex? Aren't you her friend as well as her lover? Is your self-esteem based on keeping her down? Do her achievements put you into an inappropriate competitive mode? We compete with an adversary—an opponent in a conflict! Is the woman you chose to go through life with your adversary?

Once you know who you are and where you're going, the next question will become clear: With whom will you travel on your life journey? With the first two important points figured out, the decision of who will be allowed to go with you is now *a choice*—rather than your just settling for someone no one else picked up.

Note: Of course, you already know that your choice of a significant other will account for a large percentage of happiness, or misery, during your life. Make it a <u>real</u> <u>choice that sets well with you;</u> not a decision filled with ambivalence.

NOTES

Approval and Availability

Okay… so far we've set the stage; but let's get into the thick of it. Single women over the age of 30 are not dating; they are *interviewing*. These women have experience, and have been behind the curtain to see how some relationships work. Psychological (and for some, biological) clocks begin their loud and obnoxious countdown, and women feel that they <u>need</u> to find a man… and quickly. Otherwise, an overwhelming sense of impending doom sets in, and our heroine sees herself waking up alone at 50, scratching at the fresh black hair dye from the previous night's "youth rejuvenation efforts," and shuffling over to the kitchen in her ex-boyfriend's slippers to pick out a fresh can of cat food for kitty's breakfast.

Her next move? Oftentimes, she ends up with the first guy who shows her a bit of attention. Desperation can—and usually does—lead to very poor decision-making. There's a reason he's still single and why no one else snapped him up, ladies. Keep in mind that no matter how good he looks on the dance floor or how sweetly he pulled out your chair for you on your first date, some other woman has recently told him that she was sick and tired of his bullshit.

Despite various red flags, our heroine ignores the warning signs, falls in love with a dream and commits. (Yes, it's only a dream she's fallen in love with. She doesn't really know this man from Adam's housecat. That would involve intimacy; not just lust or simple conversation under strobe lights and pounding bass notes from concert speakers.) Soon, she finds herself making all kinds of excuses for the man she chose. Whether she is a career professional or a domestic goddess, she is now listening and responding to statements she *swore* she would never hear… that at every turn limit her and stretch her sanity. Keep in mind, these statements come regardless of who the breadwinner is or if our heroine has a full-time career outside the home:

NOTES

"Get me a beer, Babe."

"Where are all my clean socks? Didn't you pick up/do my laundry?"

"What are you making for dinner?"

"Have you seen/Where did you put my _____?"
(Feel free to insert pretty much anything here: keys, watch, wallet, cell phone.)

And the capper is usually on his way, running out the door in the morning: "Have a good day, Honey. Oh! I forgot to tell you. I have to pick up John Smith from the airport tonight. Can you rustle up a really elegant dinner? It probably won't take you too long. Oh yes—make sure the kids bathe tonight, too. And I think one of the kids mentioned that there's a test tomorrow, so you need to quiz them. I'll be taking John out for drinks after dinner, so you won't have to wait up for me."

With all this to do—and all that the Man's Man takes for granted—it's no wonder that there's no time or energy to even *think* about what you might want in your life. Ladies, you are too permissive, too passive, and too available. And take a good look at men. Do we truly look like we *need* another mother? Forgive me, let me rephrase... **should we need** a "mommy" at our age?

A brief pause, dear Reader, as I need to get something off my chest and send a personal message to the demanding, self-centered, passive-aggressive remote control holders who have the same pink parts as I. (Not all of you; offenders know who they are): Get up and do these things yourself! You want some juice? Get up and get it! You want a cold beer? Get up off the sofa and get it! What's the problem? Rough day at work? Need some alone time? Give me a break. You should have had a solid idea of what she expected from living your lives together before you married her… and you've been short-changing her for a while now. Her doing nice things for you—as well as your doing nice things for her gives you both pleasure. This may be a brand-new concept for you—reciprocity. Yes, reciprocity is definitely the name of the game. You can be sure she didn't sign on to be your personal handmaiden.

I've been working for high-technology startup companies for the last 15 years, and I know the deal: 16 to 18-hour days: Zero "me time", tons of stress, and a five-hour round-trip commute; and I did—and do—my share* around the house, putting laundry away, changing diapers, performing midnight feedings, and mopping the floor—just to name a few things that have to be done in a normal household. What?? You need to put your feet up!? Look, guys, you need to recognize that marriage is a full-time job. It takes investment and effort.

Much of this will change when men start accepting accountability. And **that** will only happen when women stop mothering, defending, and enabling them. Ladies, think about it… Don't you hate being a mother to your man-child?

---

* Not to be confused with "helping my wife"; big difference! You're not doing her a favor, although men who "help" view it that way. Doing your fair share of anything clearly shows a responsibility, not an infrequent generosity on your part.

NOTES

Demanding and Bitchy

Tina, the incredible woman who did me the honor of marrying me, is bitchy. She knows it, I know it and it's a big reason why I married her. Please understand; I say this with the utmost respect and love. Evolved Men are confident and strong—much stronger than our pseudo-dominant brethren—and we need someone to "bump up against." Tina is my counterpart and equal—strong, smart, brave, and opinionated—and we work hard *together* to keep equality top-of-mind in our relationship. She desires the best we can afford in everything (materially, emotionally, and spiritually). She acts without regret, speaks her mind, and demands to be *listened to* as well as heard. She is both protagonist and antagonist in our marriage... and I wouldn't change it for the world.

Being bitchy is different than being a bitch. One of the topics women spoke about often was bitchiness. They told me clearly that they tried diligently to "keep their man in check," but that it didn't work. (I thought to myself, "No kidding.") Loud complaining does not qualify as bitchy. Bitchy could more aptly be described as a combination of feisty, demanding and expectant... all positives, as these are the things that keep couples growing together and motivated as individuals.

Bitchy women refuse to settle for mediocrity. It's not about material things; it's about respect, effort, paying attention, intimacy, and a genuine interest in life. The woman in a man's life is *equal*, regardless of who makes the money... and I say this from the standpoint of personally having stepped up—to pick up the slack in our household when my wife went back to school. We are a real team. I work full time, she goes to school and studies, and we both do everything that a house and two growing children require... **without** keeping track of who has done what, and without bickering. Men do not have the right to stifle the needs of the women in their lives.

NOTES

Partnerships—romantic or otherwise—must be founded in equality. If women want and need more, they must move beyond *asking* their significant other, and start demanding.

Demands are to be presented as clear and firm requests for action. Want more romance? Let him know that he needs to listen, or he will force you to find other avenues to fulfill your needs. I'm not suggesting having an extra-marital affair, but getting needs met is vital for any human being. After all, women are women **first**, and wives/mothers **second**. Personal needs must find a priority near the top. A man—if he truly cares about you—should and will help you fulfill your needs and attain your goals— for yourself, for your relationship, for your life.

Lead… jointly

It's all about equality and a true partnership. Do not accept what comes if it's not what you want; insist on what you need, even if you must be the one to take it yourself. Stifled women are miserable inside and suffer all sorts of health problems. That is no mere theory; it is fact. In many cultures where the great majority of women are subservient, the predictable consequence is illness. Women who don't demand more and lead *with* their partners wake up in mid-life and look back wondering what happened to their lives. This, from June in Kansas City… a story I would have **never** believed if I hadn't heard it directly from the source: "I never asked for anything more from him… I just took what he had time to provide. One day he took me to a hotel [he stayed at] on business trips. As we checked in together, the desk clerk looked at him and said, 'New secretary, huh?' I spoke with the manager, and the clerk was fired… but I just never thought he would do that. I give him everything he wants!" Through our conversation, we discovered that she did give him whatever he wanted, except she didn't demand that he treat her as an equal leader in their lives. June left her wants, needs, and self-respect completely out of the equation.

NOTES

And what does a woman show her children about self-esteem when she's under a man's thumb? For a young boy, it perpetuates the madness of abusive relationships, thus creating another mediocre woman-stifler. (And if you haven't seen a young teenage boy in your friends' house, ordering his mother around as he's seen his father do a million times—same bad tone, same obnoxious gestures—you're in for a big shock. It certainly shocked and saddened me when I observed it with one of my son's friends.) And for girls, it shows them that women must know their place... right behind their man; unseen, unheard, always outwardly supportive while long-standing hidden inner resentments eat away at their mental and physical health.

When it comes to leadership, the Old Boys' Club seems to be alive and well. The Glass Ceiling is very much in place. Although many women break through, it's there... thwarting the efforts of aspiring female leaders today. Women are, in my opinion, the most natural leaders of the world. It's very sad to say that men haven't Evolved sufficiently yet to truly accept and welcome that sector of the population more often for leadership. If you pull back the covers on the majority of households in contemporary society, who runs the house? That's right; women are most often the rulers of the roost.

I would further this brief treatise on leadership by offering my long-held, fervent belief: This great country of ours will not become whole until a woman leads it with her brains, instead of a man and his ego leading it from his bottomless well of testosterone. After all, there is irrefutable evidence—even as I write this—that many U.S. presidents, congressmen and government officials have had extramarital affairs; affairs which have led to glaring public humiliation of their wives, and scandal for themselves. The following is a bird's eye historical view of some of our nation's "leaders" and their despicable actions toward the women in their lives. I can't help but wonder... without honor at home, how much dishonesty was behind their administrations' closed doors?

NOTES

40

Without changing the focus of this book, I might add that adultery is not strictly an American phenomenon, and is certainly not peculiar to only American politicians.

- **Thomas Jefferson**: Jefferson fathered several children outside his marriage, to include (at least) one child he'd fathered with one of his slaves.

- **Grover Cleveland**: Back in 1884 after having admitted fathering an illegitimate son who had been quietly put up for adoption, Cleveland managed to barely squeak into the White House. He somehow weathered the storm of his opponents' public taunts of "Ma, ma, where's my pa? Gone to the White House. Ha-ha-ha."

- **Dwight D. Eisenhower**: Whispers about Eisenhower's extramarital relationship with his wartime chauffer Kay Summersby swirled about for years. Six years after his death, she wrote a book about their affair, but denied any sexual intimacy. President Harry Truman didn't agree…

- **John F. Kennedy**: Kennedy's insatiable appetite for women eventually became well known, in addition to his having had a penchant for walking on the wild side. There were rumors of affairs with Marilyn Monroe, and with Judith Exner, a known paramour of a Mafia don.

- **Bill Clinton**: Public sentiment was nowhere as tolerant when the Clinton/Lewinsky scandal broke. As Clinton was being impeached, some congressmen abruptly resigned, rather than risking the humiliation of public scrutiny of their dalliances.

I suppose the real question is this: How many stained interns' dresses need to be paraded in front of the world before a change is made? When will women dare to empower themselves, and

NOTES

41

forbid men from behaving and "leading" like dogs in heat? Perhaps when women take a real stand and stop sacrificing their self-worth, changes will begin to emerge.

Being a leader means being willing to be a partner concerning the little things, too. Women: How many times have you taken a walk with a man and you're one-half step behind him—even though he's holding your hand? Shouldn't both of you be holding hands and walking *together?* You're sending him a subliminal message that you need to be led, ladies. He should be walking *with* you. Red flag.

I'm not suggesting that women need to lead full time in order to be content. Most women want a man to take charge and lead at least *some* of the time—and some women would like the man in charge *most* of the time. However, when men refuse to level the playing field and count the women in their lives as equals, they quickly find that they have alienated their wives… and women find that they have unfulfilled goals and desires.

Conclusion

Women daring to tread in the world of men will find it a complicated arena. It's not enough for women to merely crave more; they must **take** more. And men must pay attention, listen, and take action—or we will continue to have failed relationship after failed relationship.

NOTES

Chapter III:
The Evolved Man Defined

Men. So full of greatness, but only a fraction of them ever achieve it. Deep-rooted, prehistoric mental motivators stimulate the majority of men: bond with a mate; protect; sire children, and ensure the survival of the species. Our society has taken that scientific knowledge, and would have us believe that because these primal urges are inextricably hardwired into the DNA of men, that information can be made to mean "Sorry, ladies, but you need to just sit back, take it, and learn to cope with men and their faults… what you see is what you get; men are the way they are. If you don't like it, change yourself to accommodate the man in your life." That's pure fiction.

And for women, for men, and for relationships, this is a no-win. We know that many women attempt to fix and change the qualities in men they find intolerable; a fruitless effort, proven by the avalanche of failed relationships. But, I most definitely do believe that men and women are capable of relating to each other differently. *Men can choose a different path.*

NOTES

I need to cut through the minutiae. An Evolved Man is not a weak-minded, fashion-obsessed, accessorized Shallowton with the charisma of a Twinkie, and a mentality that is slower than the last 10 cents of gas during a fill-up. Quite the opposite. Men who Evolve, and aspire to embrace the truly civilized side of their personalities are part of a movement; a new lifestyle, if you will. Evolved Men aren't emotionally stunted, shallow, vacant shells of pseudo-masculinity, dressed in the latest couture. They are overflowing with style, to be sure—but style alone is just an empty wrapper. A man who is genuinely involved in the process of Evolving is classy, charming, honest, and emotionally available, and has an overwhelming need to pay attention to the world around him; to be an integral part of it. Evolved Men openly love the women in their lives whether their relationship is platonic or romantic. They connect with them on strange, yet familiar ground—even sisterly—and are secure enough to admit it. They know what to say, when to say it, and to whom. They don't relate to women or other men in passive-aggressive or controlling ways. These are educated men; well-read, adoring, fashionably dressed, refined, and outrageously playful at the appropriate times. They know their lady's shoe size, and they're aware of the local and national issues of the day, what the weather will be this coming weekend, why the bottom button on a man's vest or coat shouldn't be fastened, and they might even know the difference between designs by Roberto Cavalli and those of Christian Louboutin (should their income support a taste for designer clothing).

Evolved Men are passionate about all the people and events in their lives, and they have an unquenchable lust for life itself. Whether the subject at hand is their children's college education, the presidential election, or the latest electronics trend, they approach and live life with incredible zeal. They exude passion, awareness, and knowledge—and search for more of it. They are the men who walk into a room full of people and are greeted with stares. They have a

NOTES

certain kind of charisma that transcends gender lines. And although a Man's Man will despise the very fabric from which Evolved Men's souls are woven, even the casual observer will see that that hostility emanates from envy.

An Evolved Man doesn't fit a mold. He might be married, single, gay, straight, black, white (or a shade in between), but he is not society's version of a man. Obviously, Evolved Men are male—their physical characteristics determined at the moment of conception. But it's crystal-clear that they have a certain spark that is best described as an amalgam of their feminine and masculine traits. The fact of the matter is that a *real man*, an Evolved Man is made up of many things; feelings, caring, commitment, energy, style… and has a strong passion for life. To call him a mere "man" (in the light of society's definition) discounts and devalues the Evolved Man he has become.

How did these men come to be? Special genes? Special jeans? The metamorphosis from Man-pig to manicure cannot usually be achieved without assistance of some kind, but it usually starts with an epiphany. And that realization—as trite as it may sound—is this: Life is growth. You may choose the direction in which you grow, or you may ignore your right of choice and just stagnate. I ask you, Evolved Men-in-training, where do you want to end up, and what are you willing to learn?

In an ideally civilized world, Evolved Men who listen, think, and appreciate life would not be considered special— at least not for those reasons alone; Evolved Men should be the norm… and unfortunately they're not. Men who come to a decision to become something more than what they currently are need to decide what kind of human being they are aspiring to be. Are they willing to rise to the occasion? To struggle in order to learn life concepts that are unfamiliar— unsettling, and sometimes even frightening? Are their minds open to replace their bogus version of masculinity with a

NOTES

genuine foundation upon which they can build a real man, from the inside out?

The challenges many of these men will face on their journey are formidable. Even something as benign as the word "vulnerability" can make a Man's Man skin crawl. These men grew up believing that being vulnerable to a woman is the antithesis of intelligent masculine behavior. Well, here's a news flash: In your present condition of "maleness" sans vulnerability, you are the real-life protagonist in the tale The Emperor's New Clothes.

Men... Here are a few superficial questions that won't hurt at all, and may jog your brain into thinking about things you've not deliberately thought about before:

> **Are you single?** Do you know how to iron? (Not a stupid question. I have met too many men—both prior to and during this writing—who were honest enough to admit that their principal reason for being married was their not knowing how to open a can, or prepare presentable clothes, etc. What a truly awful reason to marry.) Can you recall the meanings of various kinds and colors of flowers? (Important! Send the wrong flowers in some parts of the world, and you may, at best, be unintentionally sending Cupid messages to someone grieving the loss of a loved one, or at worst, be sending sentiments of hatred or threats!) Can you say the word *intimacy* in mixed company without cracking a joke about it? Do you recognize that intimacy doesn't have only a sexual connotation, but also means "a non-sexual emotional connectedness experienced by

people of the same sex"? Do you know the difference between a Half-Windsor and a Full-Windsor? Do you really think you'll find your soulmate if you're dressed like a twit, and you refer to women as "bitches"? When you introduce yourself to a woman, are the most original words that come to mind, "Hey, Baby. Your eyes radiate..."? Are you prepared to sweep the woman you're going to marry off her feet? Do you have enough of **you** together (read: who you are, where you're going) to offer her what she wants and needs as a woman **and** a wife?

Are you married? Do you engage in foreplay before you even enter the bedroom? (Not necessarily physically, but with words, gestures, body language, and atmosphere.) When was the last time you wrote her a love note? Do you give her flowers for no reason, or only as an apology? Do you—at the last minute—send someone else to buy the gifts you give your wife for her birthday? Do you think your wife is beautiful in the morning? Hair tousled or not... makeup on or not; the essence of her? Do you remember that your wife has needs, and that she's counting on you as her partner to help her in fulfilling them—just as she does for you? Are your eyes straying, even when she's walking right next to you? Do you want to look at your wife across the breakfast table in 5 or 10 years and say, "Damn, I gave you my best years..." only to hear her reply, "Those were your **best**?"

NOTES

Abandoning the behaviors of the male stereotype and still maintaining masculinity is learned and accomplished through careful introspection. But perhaps the most essential element to develop is the ability to pay close attention to the valuable information offered by the women in our lives. Some of these women are family members, some are friends, and some are lovers. My personal transition required a concerted effort toward listening (something *all* men have a hard time doing, and something I still struggle with at times), and then internalizing what I'd heard in order to take action. I do not believe that my wife is the sole reason for the drastic changes in my behavioral Evolution, although it's clear to me that she is the catalyst; my inspiration, my muse.

I knew very early on that I was not like the "other boys." (Similar, I suppose, to how gay men and women often say that they knew they were gay when they were very young children.) My mother told me that my profound attraction to the arts, and my natural gifts and talents for dancing, music, and acting deserved a serious investment of my time and effort; that they made me a special person. For most of my adolescent life, young women saw me as unique and alluring, while some young men—the ones whose sexual definition was still in the process of becoming integrated, as I now know—verbally accosted me with anti-gay epithets. The error in their perception of my sexual orientation was not at all disturbing; the hatred in their faces and voices was. (In retrospect, I imagine I must have had a very healthy sense of self-confidence regarding my own sexual definition. In today's society, straight boys and men hear "You're gay!", and they freak!

Judging from the feedback I received from the women I encountered on my new path to becoming an Evolved Man, I learned that their perception of me was very similar to how people viewed my father—beguiling, charismatic, quietly captivating. My attraction to women and their attraction to

NOTES

48

me was not based on something solely physical. There was an emotional *connection*; a brotherhood/sisterhood; a synergistic *partnership*, because we always wound up with what felt to us to be even greater than what we'd both invested. Women call this connection "intimacy," and long for it from the emotionally unavailable men in their lives. They use their part of the connection for giving and receiving love. But men call it "charm," and use it to get what they think they want out of a relationship: sex. Period.

Through the hundreds of conversations and interviews I've had with men and women in all walks of life—across the spectrum of income level, creed, and ethnic background— I have found that I am far from alone in these thoughts. A multitude of men (multitude, yes, but still a very small minority) understand and feel the connection I describe. They tell me they share my thoughts and feelings when they think of their relationships with their wives, their sisters, or their female friends—and they unanimously agree that it is unmistakably a feminine bond they feel. I would argue that if men could stop misinterpreting this connection—seeing it as an opportunity to charm the pants (pardon the pun) off their latest female mark—they could take the first baby-steps toward recognizing this supposedly feminine bond as a *human bond*. Men could then begin to notice how that connection makes them *feel*: complete and fully engaged with love and life. It's logical to conclude that once a man achieves this realization, his family, his friendships, his business relationships, and his commitment to a romantic relationship or marriage could finally take their rightful places as top priority in a newly-Evolved Man's life.

It is important to note that men who have Evolved and have integrated these beliefs in their daily lives, are not able to fake it. In spite of the importance of being aware of fashion and style, it would be a grave error to think that becoming an Evolved Man is as simple as buying an Armani suit, Versace

NOTES

sunglasses, and a pair of Bruno Magli shoes. Style—socially and professionally—is very important. It shows self-respect, personal pride, and attention to detail. But packaging only goes so far; eventually the "product" has to perform.

A cold and hard self-evaluation is in order for all men. Sometimes, when you stare at the looking glass, the looking glass stares back. It is through these reflections—as well as the very valuable aforementioned feedback from the women in our lives—that men can see who they are, and what they represent. It is this careful internal taking of inventory that enables men to truly change; to successfully metamorphose into Evolved Men.

NOTES

Chapter IV:
The Path to Evolution – An Evaluation

It's become more common than not for men to label civilized human qualities as abnormal qualities for a "real man" to have, simply because society views those qualities as feminine. As an Evolving—or Evolved—Man, how can you evaluate how much societal nonsense you've thrown off, and how much you've absorbed? What are your attitudes about women? About life? About style? About yourself? Find out by answering these simple questions to benchmark your current state of Evolution. You will instantly see what is lacking. You'll also see the direction in which to go to expand your awareness of culture, style, sex, and general knowledge. If you're a female reader, you can answer the questions from your point of view, regarding the man in your life. Check where he stands in the grand scheme of things. Is he up to par?

As you peruse the following questions, delve into your gray matter. Some of these questions are common sense, and some are simple, yet intuitive. Others are trivia questions that

NOTES

are by no means trivial. And some will give you some clues about the kind of love relationships you have. It is important to note that this is by no means a complete test, nor is it a scientific test. It is merely a gauge to see where things stand. Check your answers after you answer the questions. You may get interesting ideas that will help you progress on your path toward Evolution.

SENSITIVITY

For any Evolved Man, being sensitive—but strong—is a prerequisite.

1. How many "chick flicks" have you seen in the past 12 months? (*A "chick flick"—a term used by the thick-skinned—is a film that conjures up emotions that are almost always considered feminine: love, gratitude, joy, bittersweet happiness, etc., and usually has a heroine of power, intrigue, and insight, in a starring role. Good examples might be Pretty Woman, How to Lose a Guy in 10 Days, Love Actually, and Somersby.*)

   A) One or two
   B) Between two and five
   C) Six or more
   D) You lost me at "chick flick"

   Answer
   How you answered directly reflects how you view emotions, and shows your willingness to experience and expose them when there's another person in the room. When you boil things down, there are two core emotions that all feelings are derived from: love and fear. Love enables joy, trust, honesty, empathy, generosity, faithfulness, and intimacy. Fear drives anger, deceit, envy, greed, distrust, the non-disclosure of feelings, and distance.

NOTES

2. What is the correct answer to this question: "Honey, does this dress make me look fat?"

    A)   "No. It's the fat that makes you look fat."
    B)   "You look fine."
    C)   "Hang on, Hon, it's almost halftime."
    D)   "Baby, you are beautiful no matter what you wear."

Answer

This was a gimmie. If you missed this question, you should be shot. However, the *reason* letter D is correct is the important thing to capture here. Your lady *should* look good to you no matter what she wears. Otherwise, why are you with her? Whether she's had kids or not, has stretch marks or not, slight dimples or flabby abs, she is the woman you fell in love with. Did you ever stop to think about why it's okay that you can be, for example, a balding, middle-aged fatty, and why she is supposed to look like she just stepped out of a Victoria's Secret catalogue? Imperfections are what define us.

3. Have you ever gone clothes shopping with or for your lady without it being a special occasion (e.g. birthday, anniversary, Christmas, etc.)?

    A. Yes.
    B. No

Answer

I realize that the stereotypical man hates shopping, but this is a special experience a man can enjoy doing

NOTES

for the woman in his life, and for himself. It allows him to know her on a level that she can't tell you about directly, and it kills the "Do I look fat?" issue. Get into it! Make it something you're both doing together, and you'll find yourself actually enjoying it. Do you really want to be one of those men sitting snoring in a chair while "**the wife** does her shopping"?

4. When was the last time you wrote her a love letter?

<u>Answer</u>
Some men may appear to be romantics at the beginning of a committed relationship, but more often than not, their romanticism subsides after some period of time. They get "comfortable" in the relationship, and they may start taking the woman in their lives for granted. And that highlights what this question is really about: How much effort do you put into the romance part of your relationship? Important note: When writing a love letter, be sure to *write* it in longhand. Believe me; I'm not being picky. Typing it and printing it out is not even slightly similar to actually writing a love letter to the woman you love.

(Personal account: Throughout the 17+ years of being together, my wife and I have shared many holidays, birthdays, and special occasions... many celebrated with gifts: bracelets, necklaces, clothes, trips, negligees, earrings, etc. What does she remember most? What is looked upon as the unrivaled "gift of gifts"? One Valentine's Day, I went to a crafts store, and bought an unusual jar—a bit squatty, with a unique lid—and I hand-painted it. I then spent two-and-a-half weeks writing my thoughts—by hand, on little slips of paper—1,000 reasons why I love her. Each one began with "I love you because..." and was followed by one reason I love her. That jar sits on our mantle, and she regards it as the best gift she has ever received.)

NOTES

5. When was the last argument the two of you had? Who won?

Answer

Couples with love and respect for each other usually don't fight. They may do some short-term, high-decibel complaining, but they don't fight. In fact, the entire concept of "winning" fights is completely false. Fights are very damaging to relationships and occur based on a desire for: A) control, and B) the fear of being wrong and/or "defeated." ("It's not enough for him to be wrong... he must concede and admit I'm right! I must win!") The next time an argument starts to escalate, try saying, "I'm sorry. You're obviously upset and I don't want you to feel that way. Will you forgive me?" Regardless of who believes they are "right," these are magic words that begin negotiation and discussion that point toward interactive problem-solving; a win/win. C'mon, guys—we always present ourselves as logical problem-solvers, discounting women for being "too emotional". Why not recognize that when one of you has a problem, you both have it? Jointly working on solving a problem is completely different from two adversaries verbally squaring off, someone going for the jugular, and then "winning." Haven't you noticed that no one wins?? And it's really a stretch to call two critically wounded survivors "winners".

STYLE and FASHION

Yes, "style points" count. No product is complete without the right packaging. But keep in mind: Under the package "wrapper", there needs to be true intelligence/knowledge.

NOTES

6. How many pairs of shoes do you own?

    A.   One
    B.   Two
    C.   Three
    D.   Four or more (with belts to match.)

<u>Answer</u>
Footwear is an important accoutrement for any man, and Evolved Men should have a selection of shoes, apart from work boots and/or tennis shoes. Regardless of the quantity or style of shoes: Are they in good repair? Are they shined? Are they in style? And, yes, belts should match your shoes.

7. Define the following: Benefit, loofa, bangle

<u>Answer</u>

Benefit Top-end women's cosmetics company

Loofa   A rough sponge-like bathing tool used to exfoliate the skin

Bangle A round bracelet (multiples are usually worn on the wrist) or earring

8. After what calendar date do women stop wearing white shoes?

<u>Answer</u>
Labor Day

9. What are French cuffs?

<u>Answer</u>
French cuffs on a top-end shirt do not have a button closure at the end of the sleeve. Cufflinks are required to fasten the sleeves at the wrist.

NOTES

10. Explain the meaning of pousse café

Answer

The literal meaning of the French words *pousse café* is "coffee chaser." Here's a dictionary definition: "an after-dinner drink consisting of several liqueurs of different colors and specific gravities poured so as to remain in separate layers". Pousse cafés were first introduced in New Orleans in the 1840's, and have enjoyed increasing popularity over the years. Liqueurs are carefully poured in layers that should not be allowed to mix. What keeps the layers separate is their varying weights. Each layer is meant to complement the one that follows. This drink should be sipped slowly, along with a cup of coffee.

11. Why must the bottom button on a man's coat or vest be left unfastened?

Answer

This practice started in 19th century England, when King Edward VII was late getting dressed for a parade. In their haste, his valets overlooked a small detail: The king's bottom vest button was not fastened when he left his dressing room. His subjects, not wanting to correct royalty, took it as a fashion statement and followed his lead. Today, no man's suit, sports jacket, or vest should be worn with the bottom button fastened.

12. Where is Mont Blanc located?

Answer

Geographically, Mont Blanc is the highest point in France, its elevation reaching a neck-wrenching

NOTES

height of more than 15,770 feet. However, the Mont Blanc referred to here is a pen. Using a pen of quality conveys that your written word deserves as much respect as your verbal word. In this light, a Mont Blanc would most likely be located in your pocket.

INTIMACY and SEX

Sex isn't everything, but it is a part of any successful relationship. Evolved Men have learned their way around a woman's body and mind, and know that sex is more than a physical act. Sex is emotional connection, anticipation, timing, love, passion, knowledge, and confidence—perhaps combined with just a smidgen of kink.

13. Where is a woman's "G-spot"?

    <u>Answer</u>
    Not meant to turn this into a sex-ed course, but let's get this answered. The G-spot is named after Ernst Grafenbergts—the researcher who first put forth information regarding that area of the female anatomy—which is said to be the anatomical counterpart to the male prostate gland. Some experts still argue if it's "real" or not (obviously, these "experts" aren't paying attention during sex), but that's utter nonsense. Here's a map: Two inches inside the vagina and about ½" to 1" toward the front of the body. Press lightly, rotate slowly, increasing pressure when—oh, you'll know when. On a personal note: If men become adept at finding and stimulating it (at the right time, and in coordination with other activities), you will not only be loved, you will be revered.

NOTES

14. If you ask a woman to list the most important attributes she would want in a man, what would be at the top of the list?

    A) Good sense of humor
    B) Class/Culture
    C) Well-endowment
    D) Wealth

Answer

Although some women look for large ponies to ride or even larger bank accounts to access, the majority of women are looking for wit and humor—with gainful employment running a close second. Men are often regarded as funnier and more clever when they work at a steady job.

15. Who talks the dirtiest about sex: men or women?

Answer

Women not only talk more about it... they get into much more detail. Here's a hypothetical example: a date.

If a man goes on a date, his friends will quiz him the next day. The opening line of the conversation starts something like: "Hey, what's up with that girl last night? Did you get her?" If the man smiles and says he did, what always follows is: "Was she good?" Some inconsequential information might be offered here, but nothing of any true substance.

In contrast, if a woman is going on a date, she usually knows if she will be sleeping with him that night. (More often than not, her friends know, too.) The pre-date confab is likely to be peppered with many

NOTES

to-the-point comments and assumptions regarding the length of time and quality of foreplay, penis size, and more. However, on the day following the date, this group needs these all-important bits of data validated or dismissed... and the only way to do that is by getting all the information out—and I mean all of it. **Everything** is going to be discussed, measured and evaluated: the way his hands moved, what he smelled like (breath and body), how long he kissed her before moving further, eye contact, what he said and the tone he said it in, and then a blow-by-blow assessment of the all-important post-sex actions during what should have been the afterglow—"Did he fall straight asleep, talk, leave, or start Round Two?"

16. What is the longest you have gone without sex *by choice* while in a relationship, and why?

17. True or False: Sex is a key ingredient in a relationship.

Let's take #16 and #17 together, as they are related.

Answer
Sex is a healthy element in a successful relationship, but it's not the core of the relationship. Abstinence — intentional or unintentional—sometimes comes in to play, perhaps when there are other things of importance needing attention. Maybe she has a lot of stress at work, or he is consumed with the kids.

But sex isn't a one-way street. I spoke with a woman whose boyfriend treated her as his personal orgasm-provider.

NOTES

60

He expected her to provide sexual favors specifically to please *him*—sometimes in excess of four to five times a day—without so much as the benefit of a kiss as foreplay. She changed her perception after our conversation, and the dénouement of their five-year relationship came soon after our talk. She told me she felt fortunate to have been able to recognize her then-partner as the totally self-centered man he was, and to then move on to learning much more about herself.

18. Have you ever asked your significant other about what they like in bed? When was the last time such a conversation took place?

Answer

This question speaks to open communication. An honest and emotionally intimate couple should be able to talk about anything and everything. Spending time discussing likes and dislikes will not only bring the two of you closer, but will be personally enlightening. By listening and talking about what matters to her, an Evolved Man may discover a part of himself he never knew existed. Besides, as you see from the answer to Question 16, women are already having these conversations, so a man should be able to join in. However, to be prepared for the answer, keep an open mind, and do your best to leave your ego out of it. Asking a woman what her ultimate fantasy is can be dangerous. If she responds honestly—*completely*—you might not be ready for the answer that comes your way.

MANNERS, ETIQUETTE, and MORE

Knowing how to make reservations or how to act on a date is important information to have, and Evolved Men know even more.

NOTES

19. Cooking is: A) what women do B) what women want C) what men provide

Answer
Cooking is all three. Any self-respecting Evolved Man should know his way around the kitchen, not the microwave.

20. What is "The Crush"?

Answer
"The Crush" is a slang term in winemaking for harvest season, when grapes are picked and crushed.

21. What do white roses symbolize in the United States?

Answer
In the U.S., white roses symbolize purity, fidelity, and ever-lasting love. *(Author's note: Although I mentioned this in an earlier chapter, it's worth repeating: Before you send roses or other flowers to a person in a foreign country, be sure to check the meaning of the flower type and color. What is joyful in one country may well be a message of grieving in another.)*

Colored roses convey other non-verbal meanings:

Red	I love you.
Deep Red	passionate thoughts
Yellow	joy, gladness
Coral	desire
Orange	fascination, enthusiasm

NOTES

Lavender	love at first sight
Light pink	grace, gentility, admiration
Dark Pink	"Thank you."

Note: In general, pale roses of any color signify friendship.

In years past, flowers were arranged in elaborate bouquets to express thoughts, or to convey secret messages. An extensive flower language (originating in Constantinople in the 1600s) was used in England in 1716 by Lady Mary Wortley Montagu. The interest then spread to France where the book *Le Langage des Fleurs* was printed and included more than 800 floral signs and secret messages. Check it out online; it makes for interesting reading.

22. What is an aperitif? Give at least two examples.

Answer
An aperitif—from the Latin *aperire*, or "to open"—is a light, dry, low-proof alcoholic beverage meant to spark the appetite. An aperitif may be as simple as a glass of dry white wine or champagne, or can have more flair, flavor, and color like Campari or Dubonnet.

23. Wines are appreciated according to seven distinct qualitative analyses. What are they?

Answer
Appearance: A sound wine should appear clean and free of any sediment. Syrupy rivulets (called "legs") along the side of the glass suggest the wine has good body.

Aroma—or *Bouquet*—is also referred to as "nose," and refers to the smell of a wine. Swirling the wine in the glass is said to help to release the bouquet,

NOTES

which is best experienced by inhaling the scent gently.

Balance is the synchronization of all of a wine's individual characteristics.

Body is the weight and texture of a wine (content of alcohol, dissolved solids) and varies according to the type of wine.

Astringency causes the mouth to pucker.

24. How many stage productions have you attended in the last year?

Answer

As you know, cinematography is the "new kid on the block" with less than 100 years of existence. It's an outgrowth of the ancient art of the Greek stage play, which is rich in culture and history. If you haven't been to the theatre, go. If you have gone, go again. The experiences gained from a night at the theatre stay with you forever.

25. Fine cigars are stored in a _____

Answer
Humidor

26. What makes Cognac, Cognac?

Answer
Cognac is a brandy produced in the region of Cognac, France; which is to say all Cognacs are

NOTES

brandies, but not all brandies are Cognacs. What's printed on the label tells you how long it has been aged:

1 to 5 Stars, VS — a minimum of 2 ½ years

5 Stars, Supérieur — a minimum of 3 ½ years

Rare, Réserve, Vieux, VSOP — a minimum of 4 ½ years

Grande Réserve — a minimum of 5 ½ years

Extra, XO, Vieille Réserve, Napoléon, Très Vieux — a minimum of 6 ½ years

GENERAL KNOWLEDGE and OTHER STUFF

Evolved Men are always expanding their knowledge of… everything!

27. What is a pentameter? (pen TAM uh ter)

<u>Answer</u>
In poetry, a pentameter is the meter used in a line of verse. Iambic pentameter is most commonly used in verse writing, and when read aloud it naturally follows a beat. In written form, the rhythm looks like this:

*da-**DUM** da-**DUM** da-**DUM** da-**DUM** da-**DUM***

To quote Lord Alfred Tennyson:

To **strive**, to **seek**, to **find**, and **not** to **yield**.

NOTES

28. Who wrote the 1812 Overture?

Answer

Written in 1880, the 1812 Overture in E Flat Major, Op. (Opus) 49 is probably Piotr Ilyitch Tchaikovsky's best-known work.

29. What is onomatopoeia? Give two examples.

Answer

Onomatopoeia is a word that imitates the sound it represents. Examples abound: buzz, hiss, clap, crash, and squish.

30. What is a palindrome? Give two examples.

Answer

A palindrome is a word or phrase that reads the same way when it's read from the end of it to the beginning, as it does when it's read normally, from beginning to end. There are many palindromes, but besides the most common one-word instances (dad, mom), some examples are: "race car"; "Sad? I'm Midas!"; "Yawn a more Roman way."

31. What, exactly, is blood pressure? What do the numbers stand for?

Answer

Blood pressure is the pressure against the walls of your blood vessels. The two numbers are usually written as a fraction, such as 120/80—read aloud as "one twenty over eighty". The first number is a

NOTES

measurement of the pressure against the walls of your blood vessels when your heart is pumping blood out to your organs—systolic pressure. The second number is a measurement of the pressure against the walls of the blood vessels when your heart is between beats and resting— diastolic pressure.

32. How are diamonds graded?

<u>Answer</u>
Diamonds are graded according to the four Cs: Color, Clarity, Cut, and Carat. When purchasing a diamond for an engagement ring, there are plenty of men/books/experts/New Age nincompoops who tell you that love makes the marriage, not the ring. This is absolutely true; if she loves your diamond and not you, the diamond is forever... and it is **you** that has a limited shelf life. However, if you are going to take the plunge, do it right. As an Evolved Man, you should expect the standard cost to be three months salary (minimum).

33. Have you read some of these books?

❑ <u>The Art of War</u> by Sun Tzu

❑ <u>Kitchen Confidential</u> by Anthony Bourdain

❑ <u>How to Argue and Win Every Time</u> by Gerry Spence

❑ <u>Fire in the Belly</u> by Sam Keen

NOTES

❑ <u>Men Are From Mars, Women Are From Venus</u> by John Gray, Ph.D.

❑ <u>The Skeptical Environmentalist</u> by Bjorn Lomborg

❑ <u>Eight Weeks to Optimum Health</u> by Dr. Andrew Weil

❑ <u>When Will Jesus Bring the Pork Chops?</u> by George Carlin

❑ <u>The Rise and Fall of the Third Chimpanzee</u> by Jared Diamond

❑ <u>The Da Vinci Code</u> by Dan Brown

❑ <u>The Dark Tower</u> by Stephen King

❑ <u>Idiom Savant: Slang As It Is Slung</u> by Jerry Camarillo Dunn

❑ <u>What Do They Say When You Leave The Room?</u> by John Waters and Brigid McGrath Massie

❑ <u>The Long Walk to Freedom</u> by Nelson Mandela

❑ <u>The 7 Habits of Highly Effective People</u> by Stephen Covey

❑ *Games People Play* by Eric Berne

❑ *Why Elephants Have Big Ears* by Chris Lavers

❑ *The Path to Love* by Deepak Chopra

NOTES

Answer

This list is just a *very* small sampling of quality works any Evolved Man should have read, or might currently be reading. A "full list" would be impossible, but would include classic works as well as those written by fine authors of modern times. Your quest for quality literature should be unquenchable. Read!

ADVANCED TRIVIA

34. What is the final word in Edgar Allan Poe's *The Raven*?

    Answer
    "Nevermore."

35. What are the names of the two cities in *A Tale of Two Cities*?

    Answer
    London and Paris

36. What is the name of the three-headed dog that guards the entrance to Hades?

    Answer
    Cerberus

37. What is the Mona Lisa called in Italian?

    Answer
    La Gioconda

NOTES

38. What three weapons are used in fencing?

Answer
Foil, saber, and épée.

39. What is the only NFL team to have had an undefeated season?

Answer
Miami Dolphins in 1972.

40. What is the highest possible score for a cribbage hand?

Answer
29

41. Which of the Great Lakes has the smallest area?

Answer
Lake Ontario

42. What character on *The Simpsons* has three nipples?

Answer
Krusty the Clown

43. What is the longest river in Europe?

Answer
The Volga River in Russia, approximately 2,500 miles long.

NOTES

44. Which two films won 11 Oscars?

Answer
Ben-Hur and Titanic

45. What is the name of the estate in Citizen Kane?

Answer
Xanadu

Thus endeth The Evaluation. How did you fare? Obviously, this is far from a comprehensive examination, but it will assist you in ascertaining your place (or your significant other's place) in just one area of the Evolutionary scale. The answers to most of these questions are available in everyday life…that is, if you pay attention… and have a thirst for new information. The real point is to get some idea of how Evolving men pay attention in their lives—to themselves, to the world around them, and to their significant other. My hope is that this is just the beginning of your journey—a life-long quest to achieve a more Evolved state of being.

NOTES

Chapter V:
For Women: How To Positively Affect A Man's Evolution... Without Losing Your Individuality

So, where do Evolved Men come from? Surely these men aren't sitting around darning socks, watching episodes of *Queer Eye for the Straight Guy*, and waiting for a woman to fall in love with them. Although the answer is not as straightforward as one would hope, some common trends can be seen through the romantic murk. A man at the start of his Evolution doesn't know what he doesn't know. Some men wake up each day with an unquantifiable sense of loss; a loss of something they never really had—a yearning for something they think they want. He knows he's missing something, but doesn't know what... and it is that feeling of not knowing that is the start of his journey.

Should an Evolving Man continue down the path of emotional growth (either through self-motivation or external influences), he will begin to understand what nags at him. He's been missing a *self*—a core built on something far more profound than the perceived success that comes from

NOTES

controlling things and people in his immediate surroundings. He may then start to recognize that if he improves himself internally, the world around him becomes a better, friendlier place... a place he hasn't truly seen before. It begins to dawn on him... he's been trading his *self* for a false sense of control.

But the question remains: Where do these men come from? My personal journey has been one of self-evaluation and introspection, turbulent change, and external motivation. And it all began with a simple realization that I wanted to be a better man. Many of the men I've spoken with have had a similar starting point for their journey, and the consensus is that successful Evolution for men is made up of a few key components:

- Doing the "real work"—an *honest* evaluation of his persona

- Having a plan of action with which to phase out the challenged components of his mental and physical self, while preparing to receive/develop new, positive elements

- Learning how to cultivate an appreciation of what is around him—both positive and negative.

However, this kind of growth usually cannot be achieved alone; that's where women can assist in the process. However, it's important to me to make one thing abundantly clear: **It is not a woman's job to "make" a man grow and Evolve.** A man's journey starts from *within himself.* **He** has to see the need to alter his behavior, his outlook, and his focus in order to be re-educated. In all honesty, men need training.

In addition to the familiar "Basic Training" in the military, "training" is something that is done all the time... with ourselves and with others. Anytime a child brushes their

NOTES

teeth without being asked, or a woman kisses her husband before she leaves on a business trip, or a man brings his wife flowers only once a year on Valentine's Day, it shows certain habits having been developed through training. But the kind of training I'm discussing here is on a much deeper level.

For many women, dealing with a man's need for training can be very frustrating. The sad truth is that many women train men each day that they're involved in the relationship. They just may not be aware of it, consciously. And unless the man is ready to change, any and all efforts to train him will fall on deaf ears. This power struggle can then culminate in a combination of fighting, hurt feelings, dissatisfaction, and ultimately separation. It's important to note, however, that training a man can eventually pay off, but possibly not in the way women might envision it.

Some of the talks I had were with women-only groups; women who ranged in age from 18 to 67 years old. They gave me their views about quite a number of important things concerning their personal and professional lives. Some of the most thought-provoking and insightful exchanges dealt with their past romantic relationships. I asked if they knew where these former boyfriends were today in their lives. For one thing, I wanted to know if these men had subsequently established permanent committed relationships. I also wanted to know what opinion the women had of these men now. In other words, did they think these men were the same as they'd been before? Kinder? More considerate, or less so? Dedicated and faithful to the women in their lives?

More than 70% of the participants had kept in touch with their first loves, so the conversation was always peppered with nostalgia and hypothesizing about what could have been. My primary interest during these talks centered on their earliest "real" boyfriend—most often referred to by the participants as "the guy I was with in college," or "my high school sweetheart." We discussed how they had met

NOTES

the man they didn't marry, the quality of their relationship, and how it ended. These were very valuable discussions. As we talked, we uncovered a lot of issues and red flags they felt they should have paid attention to. They then recounted the break-up and the aftermath of the break-up of their first relationship.

Many of these women had good things to say about where their first loves had ended up... even 10–20 years after the fact. Most were not bashing them, but instead seemed almost wistful, highlighting how these guys now seemed to be dedicated fathers... faithful husbands... more romantic... less angry... I explained to them that they had taught the men how to start and maintain a strong relationship. In effect, these women laid the groundwork for someone else's happiness. Their ex-boyfriends had been offered training by these women, and took that training to their new relationship where another woman was reaping the rewards.

"Well then, where the fuck is the man that someone else is training for me?" asked Rochelle from San Francisco. We all laughed. I told her that she most likely wasn't very far off. When it comes to romance and relationships, most men seem to be experiential learners—learning and making mistakes along the way, and getting better the more they do it.

The majority of men below a certain level of Evolution are not emotionally engaged in a relationship at all. As such, they end up breaking hearts and moving on. As they fail, they learn... slowly. As they gain experience, they integrate more and are better prepared for a meaningful relationship. As a man gets it straight in his head and starts to Evolve, he may meet a woman he really does care for; a woman who provides the impetus for a big growth spurt in his Evolution. But, where does that leave the women he left in his Evolutionary wake?

NOTES

In order to solve the problem and not just treat the symptoms, men need to learn a better way; but women have just as much to learn. To recap: Men's issues are at the root of the problem, but the women in their lives can help stop the cycle... **when they help themselves.** Both men *and* women must change their modus operandi, and there are no short cuts; men must start down the path of Evolution themselves. Women—*by staying true to their own needs and wants and not sacrificing their individuality and self-respect—* will help themselves as much as they help men. There are no losers. The worst-case scenario? The man refuses to Evolve, and leaves her because "he can't handle the pressure". The woman now has to come to grips with building the self-esteem she's never really had. Not an easy task, particularly after suffering a deep rejection. One consolation: She's now free to invest all her energy into her own self-growth. The hope is that with a lot of persistence, she will eventually find herself in a mental place where there is empowerment, focus, clarity, and confidence aplenty.

Evolution

Let's face it: Men are a mess. Unattached and un-Evolved men are usually very comfortable with who they are. They do what they want when they want, and how they want. But things radically change once a man becomes romantically involved. At the beginning of a relationship, men go above and beyond in their efforts to listen, please, help, and participate—romantically, physically, and monetarily. However, once he has put in the initial effort and his needs start being met, his behavior changes and that extra effort he's been putting out quickly dissipates. He then starts providing the bare minimum required to achieve the same result. Why? In a word: control. Here's the faulty way of thinking, right from the horses' mouth:

NOTES

As the novelty of a new relationship wears off and reality sets in, a man feels a profound sense of loss: **of control**, of individuality/identity, of freedom, and of his *self*.

> "Why do I have to check in with her?"
>
> "I need some space on the weekends. She's smothering me."
>
> "Why does she start bitching at me the second I walk in the door?"

Therefore, to achieve the balance he thinks he needs so desperately, he dominates the woman and does not *allow her* to control anything. She has a place, to be sure, but it is the place he affords her... his constant goal being to keep that place within his control. With over 80% of divorcees citing "irreconcilable differences" as the reason for divorce*, conscious or subconscious struggle for control seems to be the cause of the majority of today's break-ups, separations, and divorces. There must be a different way.

* Association for Divorce Reform, 2004

Understanding the Dilemma

For a woman to participate in a man's Evolution, she must understand the definitions of control, emotional vulnerability, and true partnership. Control and emotional vulnerability are very complicated issues for people in general—and men in particular—crossing over into a number of areas: work, children, sex, decision-making, conversation, friendships, and more. Anything to do with keeping control and preventing emotional vulnerability is a highly-calculated emotional expenditure—even if it's done at an unconscious level. If—for some unfathomable reason—men lose control, they *must* get it back immediately.

But these thought-processes are flawed. Men live under the delusion that control is 100% theirs; this is simply not

NOTES

true. In actuality, women **allow** men to control things. Now, I know what some of you are thinking: "What are you **talking** about, you nut? The man in my life is **domineering and controlling**! He hoards his money (but spends whatever he wants on himself), and he demands **so** much: 'Do! Do! Do! And when you're done, **do some more!**'"

Sorry, but the truth is that men are very vulnerable; fragile, in fact… most having *very* weak egos that are built on all the wrong things—control/dominance, sexual prowess, monetary success… even the number of beers they can drink in an hour. The quintessential example: If a woman verbalizes her dissatisfaction with a man's sexual performance—or performance as a wage earner—he's cut to the quick, and never really recovers. My polls show that a large percentage of women agreed on two things: 1) They were frequently dissatisfied in bed… and 2) They would **never** tell the man in their life how they felt about his bedroom performance (or lack thereof), for fear of "killing him." I certainly understood why they felt as they did. I explained, "Men have exquisitely-sensitive egos, and have been horribly programmed from childhood. They've been brought up to think that they know everything a woman wants without her saying a word, and that as real men they're **entitled** to dinner waiting on the table; that they are in control, full-time."

Control issues are everywhere, and men bring their emotional baggage to the scene. Because the major part of a man's ego is based on how well he performs in bed, let's look at one sexual act for a moment: the blowjob.

Now, look; I am not about to field a bunch of e-mail from women about how oral sex is evil, or from men about how I'm screwing up their sex lives. Let's get this out of the way: Sex and all things to do with sex are great. I'm not talking about how to perform a blowjob; I'm talking about the *motivation* for doing it—why he wants it, and why she wants to do it.

NOTES

Picture it: There he is on his back, arms stretched out, eyes closed, completely at the woman's mercy—with the most sensitive part of his anatomy exposed and defenseless, not to mention that it's placed in an area where it could be severed from his body. This is a man in control? Of course not. **He is 100% devoid of control**. This sexual act is the epitome of physical and emotional vulnerability.

And what do women get out of it? First off, women are much more in touch with their feelings, and relate better to love and trust during times of sexual intimacy. Secondly, women like to please—not in a negative, contrived way, but in a positive, endearing way. (read: "I love him, so whatever he likes makes me—and us—happy.") Besides, the truth is: The penis is not an attractive appendage. As Loren in Norfolk, VA observed, "It even sounds bad... like something hanging off the end of your toe... 'Oh! Ouch! I stubbed my penis!' It's so ugly!"

So, why do men pretend to be totally invulnerable, and carry that attitude into the bedroom? Two reasons: 1) Society has defined sex as "correct" only when the man is dominant, and most definitely **not** vulnerable; and 2) Men's behavior shows an odd unawareness of the subliminal meanings behind their vulnerability, and women seem to be just as peculiarly unaware.

The anecdote I just gave is just one example of the control issues men struggle with. There are many others—both in and out of the bedroom. For instance, whenever he says one thing and does another; when he tells you part of a story and leaves out "incriminating" sections about himself; whenever he mutters something under his breath but won't repeat it when you ask, "What did you just say!?", he's projecting false strength, and acting disrespectful in a vain attempt at gaining the upper hand. Let's examine another issue that exemplifies men's need for dominance over women: the toilet seat.

NOTES

Men think they are 100% straight shooters. Even if we want to believe that the majority of men have perfect aim (which is NOT true), it's clear that they haven't made the quantum leap necessary to understand the difference between a latrine—which is by definition, a toilet used only by men—and a bathroom that's in one's home, to be used by everyone who lives in the house, as well as by any visitor. Whether men agree with the following statement or not, nothing can change the reality of it: **Leaving the toilet seat up is a clear statement of control and power**. Somehow, men have designated themselves as "owner of the toilet seat", and have made its "normal" position open—and up. And the problem doesn't stop with men. Our Man's Man perpetuates the problem by showing his kids (from the time they've been toilet trained) that when a woman wants to use **his** toilet seat, she must first put the seat down, every single time she needs to use it. Here's a scenario played out in millions of homes: It's 2:00 am.... She's pregnant... groggily awakens to go to the bathroom, and doesn't turn the light on. Upon sitting, she's not groggy anymore! She just sat on a cold, wet (with his urine!) porcelain toilet base, and may have also wet her bottom with the water that's in the toilet. (Did he also forget to flush it?)

To an even further extreme, there is this example from Maria in Houston, TX: "He woke me in the middle of a cold night, and insisted I get out of bed **to sit on the toilet seat** and **warm it** for him!!" And did she? I'm so sorry to report that she said she did. Some men's need to dominate has no bounds... and many women suffer horribly from the childhood programming they received from their families... (read: A woman's primary role is to serve her family, to the exclusion of her own needs.)

Control struggles like these damage self-esteem, and it's women—in their constant effort to improve/change/save the relationship—who consistently take in the most emotional

NOTES

81

damage as they try to adjust and change themselves to become "acceptable." To change these conditions, women need to take back control... and by doing so, they can clearly demonstrate to men how to provide what they want and need. No mixed signals, no misinterpretations, and no wondering; just clear, respectful demands for what they need as *women*. Men need to be held 100% accountable for their actions by the women in their lives; women need to hold the line, and not allow men to behave like bratty children, in their attempts to get away with controlling everything.

My study bears out the findings of a multitude of researchers: Matters regarding sex, finances, child-rearing, and household chores top the long list of tension topics where women feel either left out, taken advantage of, discounted, forced to comply/cooperate, or completely removed from any decision-making process. Without a doubt, these issues are symptomatic of control. As one looks at those problems, the heart of the matter is quickly revealed: the totally lack of equality in committed relationships. In actuality, equality is a key ingredient of any marriage, relationship between colleagues, romantic relationship, or platonic friendship of any stripe: male/female, female/female, male/male. My reasoning behind this (apart from the obvious) is straightforward: Relationships are not born fully formed and functioning; individuals with desire, opinions, and needs build them... organically. For a relationship to be successful, the needs of both individuals must be addressed, because those needs impact every aspect of the relationship. This is a partnership; an Equal Relationship.

NOTES

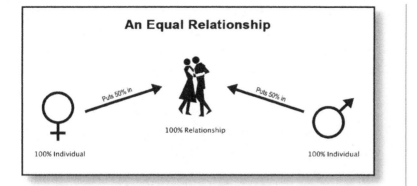

A relationship can be forged with love and respect as the main components. The relationship is equal in that each individual puts 50% of himself/herself into it. This serves two purposes: 1) 50% from each individual creates a 100% Equal Relationship; and 2) Each individual still retains 50% of himself/herself. Should the unfortunate occur and the relationship fall apart, neither of them would lose who they are—**the core** of their identities. This is obviously a perfect scenario. (The unfortunate reality is that people go into relationships with their past experiences and emotional baggage in tow—and haven't worked on their own "stuff".) By mutually investing in the creation of an Equal Relationship, couples can potentially ameliorate the corrosive effects of past damage, and begin to create trust and intimacy.

To further explain the dynamics, let's consider a common relationship/marriage issue in which control and equality play a part: "Home Operations" (Household chores, food shopping, finances, discipline of children, helping them with homework when necessary...)

Women are very angry about the man's passive-aggressive way of "helping" around the house. To quote Joan, in Syracuse, who talked about a **very** common scenario: "...whatever chores he helps with are done badly, or left half-done... left for me to come up behind him to finish properly." By doing things in a very mediocre fashion, Joan's husband

NOTES

was pushing her into the role of "army sergeant," with her inspecting and then angrily criticizing his "help." Maybe he does this by design—perhaps on a subconscious level, perhaps not—but on some level, hoping for her to angrily throw up her hands and say, "Forget it. It's easier to just do it myself." A perfect "lose/lose" situation. In the example I just gave, the response from Joan's husband is predictable: "Fine; you do it. I guess you know everything. If you don't like the way I do something, do it yourself."

Obviously, situations like these are not workable. To counter this, women need to put themselves into the process by practicing the three simple steps to take back control. And... they need to train the men in their lives.

Three Simple Steps

I'm sure you've heard the maxim "Things get worse before they get better," and a woman choosing to take back control of her own life may serve as a prime example. Always keep in mind, though, that a woman isn't really taking anything *away* from the man, per se, although his behavior clearly shows he feels she is. She is merely *taking back her portion* of the control she had ceded; nothing more. Granted that this is most likely a very unnatural state of affairs in their relationship, as she may have given over control of her life to him years earlier.

Step One: Distance

The quickest way to have a man take notice is *for her to ignore him.* It sounds simple, but it is extremely effective (and to remind you, dear Reader... I do speak from experience.) Please note that this technique shouldn't be confused with "The Silent Treatment"—a strategy meant as punishment that usually derives from an angry emotional state, and is only good for starting—or continuing— an argument.

NOTES

84

Here's the secret: In order for a man to feel in control, he needs to be the center of his universe. (Translation: He needs the woman in his life to see *him* as the center of *her* universe.) Once it becomes clear to him that the tide has shifted and that some of her attention is elsewhere, the man will perk up and take notice. The distance she creates *needs to be genuine;* not spiteful nor aggressive, no head trips, psychological games...no hidden agenda with the goal of inciting an argument. The purpose is to truly enable the woman to get into herself and her needs—to think about activities she likes/wants/has longed to do that don't include the man in her life. This is probably new territory for her, as years may have passed since she's dedicated time to thinking about herself, her dreams and goals *away* from a boyfriend, husband, or family. Clearly, this isn't about filling up her life with a long list of meaningless activities to the point that would leave no time at all for him... or them. It could be something basic—like her need for space—time alone on a vacation, a hobby she's always wanted to learn, or something as simple as reading a book.

Men do not respond well to being put off, and it won't be long before the man becomes insecure and demands an explanation re: where her attention and/or time is going. Once this occurs, the woman can further her control over the situation, thereby gaining ground. Stephanie in Los Angeles, started these steps and was shocked at how fast her husband reacted: "I started taking a stenography course at night and made some new friends. A few nights a week we would grab coffee after class... and after the first week, he started asking me why I was having an affair. I wasn't! I was just doing something for myself!" I explained that her husband was merely pulling out all the stops to get control back and have her "prove" her devotion... and might even go so far as to ask her to quit the class. She recognized the signs, too, and she stayed vigilant. And... are they still married? Stephanie's e-mail stated that they are, and that things—and

Notes

85

her husband—have changed for the better. Oh... and yes, he had tried telling her to prove she wasn't having an affair by quitting the class.

And this brings up a key point: Creating distance will most likely start an argument—or a series of arguments, and this should be expected. Control is a valuable commodity in any relationship, and simply asking for it doesn't mean that the request will automatically be "granted." Control is much like independence, which must be *assumed*; it is not usually given freely. Women achieving success in this step will find their men confused, insecure, and generally unsure of where the relationship is headed.

Step Two: Assertiveness

The man is now on the defensive, and his self-confidence is somewhat shaken. Step Two involves the woman continuing to assert herself in order to gain a stronger hold on control, and to drive equality through the relationship. This is the time to clearly spell out wants and needs in a matter-of-fact, non-confrontational fashion; concisely and *calmly*. It's virtually guaranteed for angry demands to be met with resistance. In addition, it's important to recognize that a person who is angry is **out of** control. There is a much higher probability that firm, unambiguous, and concise statements will eventually be heard.

Step Two is fundamentally about assertive negotiation, and convincing your partner of the extreme importance of recognizing your needs, rather than giving him ultimatums. It's important to mention that this process takes time. (Ever attempt to box-train a cat? Did it work the first time?) Careful phrasing and calm discussion from the woman is paramount ... and the key to this is to "get on the man's side." That should not be understood to mean that she must agree with him, or "fold" (read: be cowed into silence when

NOTES

she encounters his opposing views). Her job in this step is to plant an idea—*a thought-seed*—in his head, and then to add to that idea on a daily basis. The premise behind this tactic is simple: It's a lot easier to convince people of things if *they* think they thought of it first. By germinating new thoughts that lead to new actions, she can effectively create an atmosphere of healthy change. Under those conditions, it's more likely that the man will think he had those new ideas all along. From there, consistency and follow-through will fortify her efforts.

Thought-seeds are very important. They point up the need in relationships to communicate on a different level. To speak respectfully to each other, couples need to learn communication techniques that are very foreign to them. A totally different way of talking, especially during the times they feel very intense—or really angry about something they want from their partner that hasn't been forthcoming. These examples should provide a starting point;

Examples of Thought-Seeds

In the past, a woman might have said:	Instead, try:	For a better reaction:
"Do you think I'm a servant in this house? I work, too, and I do EVERYTHING! Try doing the dishes once in a while."	"I'm tired and I know you are, too. Do you want to wash or dry?"	A response the woman controls. While not forcing the man with an ultimatum, this statement provides the illusion of choice, and has a positive expected outcome: completion of the project without the woman doing all the work.

NOTES

"Don't you care about career advancement? How about putting in as much effort at your job as you do on the remote control?"	"You've been working at your job for [XX] years now; I think you're great at what you do. Aren't you due for a raise soon? You know you really deserve one."	This statement accomplishes two things: 1) It communicates that the woman is proud of her mate's career. (That's something men really need to know, particularly if she makes more money than he does.) 2) If the man is indifferent about his employment, he will feel the respect and admiration in her words, and possibly feel a renewed enthusiasm for his career.
"How many dinners do I have to prepare before you do some of it, too? Don't give me that 'I can't cook' stuff. Learn! I had to!"	Take a couples' culinary class. Cooking ends up fun, instead of being a chore.	He'll participate in the kitchen more, and cooking often leads to other things with more heat, and less clothes.
"Stop asking me stupid questions about where your stuff is! Am I your Thomas Guide? I have enough to keep track of without keeping tabs on your wallet/keys/ cell phone, etc."	Pick a specific place in the house (preferably on his side of the dresser) and buy a nice box or tray. Announce that this is his space for his things and put all of the items there.	Men like to have a designated area that's theirs, no matter how small. If something is designated as His Domain, he will use it. If he doesn't, gentle ribbing if/when he loses something is all that is necessary.

NOTES

"I am tired of laundry. Your turn."	Try a "Movie and Laundry Night"	A lousy chore that most people hate gets done quite well when it's being shared…and with a bit of fun, too—when you throw in a few DVDs.
"Don't talk to me like that! I'm not your bitch."	"Your tone of voice is so disrespectful. I won't speak to you until you talk to me with the same respect you want for yourself."	This most often leads to a period of silence, followed by an apology from the man. In the long term, this can also lead to changed male behavior, if she's consistent.

The process is not easy. It takes quite a bit of effort, but it works. Further, it takes concentration, resolve, and above all… *patience*. Note that these changes in **how** you say things won't yield instant results. More time, effort, and patience may be needed.

Step Three: Consistency and Follow-Through

Consistency and repetition are basic ingredients for promoting change in a man's behavior… and this is where the rubber meets the road. Oftentimes, women start the process and sail through the first two steps, but they don't stay consistent and follow through. Much like when governing children, choose only the truly important limits and boundaries to be set in stone, and never back down. In the case of dealing with children: If the child recognizes weakness, he/she will then run roughshod over all the rules of the house. Women need to use the same relentless consistency and limit-setting with

NOTES

men, if change is to occur. They must stay vigilant and strong, or a return to Step One will be the only option available to them. If Step Three is to be truly successful, it's important that issues and battles be picked carefully; not every little thing needs to be corrected and/or changed. Men are human beings, and as such their individuality must be considered.

Through risk can come reward, although there are no guarantees. Don't give up on the process if at first you get negative reactions; Men are challenging creatures to deal with. Through his eyes, he may see the road to enlightenment as treacherous, lengthy, and just too hard to walk. Women shouldn't **ever** think they are doing the wrong thing by promoting change. If they were truly happy, felt valued, and were treated as equals in their relationships, this process would not be necessary.

If these three simple steps are followed, you will see one of two outcomes; both positive!:

1. The man will adjust the mannerisms and habits (albeit gradually) that have been the death knell of the relationship, thereby transforming the relationship into a true partnership with control shared between both parties. **OR,**
2. The man will not change, but the woman is empowered with a new sense of control over her own life, and has learned to be self-reliant.

Training a man is not an easy task, but the rewards can be great. Most men are capable of so much more, but don't know it. Some men simply lack the proper motivation. I ask women to stop focusing all their attention on changing themselves to become acceptable to the man in their lives, but rather to firmly guide them. I ask men to open their minds to the possibility that they don't know as much as they think they do. With the right woman *at his side*, a man's world can be so much greater than he had ever imagined.

NOTES

90

Insight into Training

An important note on training men when they're at the start of their Evolution: As women engage the men in their lives and attempt these methods of training, they need to realize that all their efforts may be for the benefit of the "next woman." Of course, that isn't the desired outcome, but it is one distinct possibility. To wit: Alvin Toffler wrote the Best Seller *Future Shock* in 1970,. With matter-of-fact conviction he wrote of "trial" or "temporary marriages"—first marriages of young people, lasting three months to three years; and of "serial marriages" that would take place after the dissolution of the "trial marriage," happening at specific turning points in people's lives. Toffler accurately predicted the coming trends, and could see how men and women would begin to view marriage as a temporary state of being.

A word about women with faulty life-scripts: Women who are "life-time man-trainers" repeatedly find the same type of man, all of whom have the same types of problems— and then they try to change/fix them. This is a pattern that needs to be broken. It's a damaging pattern that speaks to the dysfunction in the woman, not to the core flaws in the man, and certainly is not the road to happiness.

NOTES

Chapter VI:
Everything You Wanted To Know About Evolved Men (But Were Afraid To Ask)

From yoga to health to literature, Evolved Men are required to invest in their minds, bodies, and souls on a daily basis. Once a man starts down the path of Evolution, his zest for life and love will increase, and his views on the world and the people around him will change. What's involved? A subscription to *GQ Magazine*? A membership at a health club? A degree from Harvard? No one can give an Evolving Man a prescription to put him on the "correct" life path. Evolution is "an inside job"… Just cast off the "Man's Man" mentality, and you will find the right enlightened life-path that fits you.

Evolved Men work hard to hone their listening skills. Being emotionally available to another person isn't about solving his/her problems (which men **love** to attempt). It's about listening, empathizing, and discussing. As you fully integrate these communication skills, you will see your relationship begin to improve.

NOTES

So where do you start to improve yourself? There are many things to address, but let's start at "knowledge and information."

LITERATURE

Knowledge is key. An Evolved Man should be well-versed in a wide variety of subjects—information gleaned from a wide variety of sources. Each day, a seasoned Evolved Man should have the latest news headlines, sports scores, and weather report at the mental-ready. Keep up to date regarding current issues, e.g., world politics, legal, financial, business, and technology. Industry-specific news regarding your career of choice is important for you to know, apart from possibly being useful in your relationships.

Reading novels, novellas, and non-fiction books that are on the New York Times Bestseller List is of great importance for any Evolved Man. Also, independent book publishers provide exposure for talented, but unknown writers. (It's akin to college football providing a public arena to players who are consumed with the desire to win; clearly an attitude that's the direct opposite to that of so many professional football players who are consumed with the desire to get paid...more and more and more. Please forgive the aside; my disappointment in some sports figures just unexpectedly welled up and spilled over...) An Evolved Man should keep some independent works—as well as mainstream works—on his nightstand. Be sure to seek out ancient works of poetry, world history, and Americana, in addition to the hard-boiled mystery or crime novel you just bought. Poetry is amazingly useful in starting conversations, and can provide the start of off-the-beaten-path conversation for a quiet picnic at the lake, or can set the mood to allow G-strings to loosen— as the case may be. A fully Evolved Man should plan on spending at least one day a month at a bookstore to soak in the latest—and greatest—of the written word.

NOTES

TV, Radio, Dailies, and Periodicals

In my opinion, most of today's TV and radio newscasts don't provide anything that resembles objective and honest reporting, although some stations are more dedicated to truth in reporting than others. The media is beholden to the advertising mega-corporations. A hard copy or online subscription to daily news sources that are less biased is mandatory for men in their quest to Evolve. *The New York Times,* the *Los Angeles Times,* the *Chicago Sun/Times,* and the *Wall Street Journal* may give you some clarity on current world issues (but, of course, strictly from the point of view of the United States) without the sensationalistic yellow journalism that's so commonplace in the media. It's wise to also read editorials from the U.K., to attempt to balance the biases, and perhaps you'll come up with something somewhat closer to a true picture of what's happening in the world. Staying abreast of current news items, sports trades, and stock index values will keep you in the know, and enable you to be a source of timely information for family, friends, and business acquaintances.

General Knowledge

Evolved Men know that reading is much more than just a way of acquiring knowledge, or of attempting to impress people by quoting obscure passages from well-known books. Some obvious benefits of reading are that it improves the mind, and promotes pride in oneself. Apart from those important benefits, it is now known that not possessing a common body of knowledge that is shared with others will have negative consequences in the business and social world. This concept has been proven by E. D. Hirsch, Jr., Joseph F. Kett, and James Trefil, who undertook the monumental task of documenting an enormous amount of information, specifically pointed at Americans; a *required body of knowledge* every American coming out of school should have—in order

NOTES

to make us a country of "culturally literate" people. What gave rise to the writing of *The Dictionary of Cultural Literacy* (now in its third edition) was their recognition of the grave lack of shared information among people working in middle management of American corporations. This book is a must-have for any Evolved Man.

LANGUAGE

Perhaps nothing is more annoying to a woman than making eye contact with an attractive, well-dressed man, watching him approach, and then hearing something as eloquent as, "Wussup, baby? Damn, you're hot! Wanna hook up, and shit?" I realize that poor use of the English language is a pet peeve of mine, but women do not respond to this type of nonsensical bullshit, either.

Conversation is more than the enunciation of sounds and syllables. Speaking—whether banter, barter, or broadcast—is an art unto itself. Phrasing and timing play heavily into the desired results, and experimentation, study, and experience will lead Evolved Men on their journey. Take your time or take a class. But whatever the choice, Evolved Men know what to say and when to say it. Experiment, learn, and expand your working knowledge of the English language.

Tenses

Proper verb tenses ~~is~~ *are* a huge problem for many, many people. (See how annoying that is?) Evolved Men-in-training, please take the time to speak in the correct tense. You don't need a degree in English, nor is it necessary to memorize all of the rules in *Strunk and White* (although a copy of *The Elements of Style* by Strunk and White can be a valuable reference book to have in your personal library.) All that's required is a sincere dedication to expressing oneself decently... a true respect for accurate communication. It

NOTES

takes concerted effort to cast off the vapid vocabulary of endless buzzwords and wrong tenses that now masquerade as "communication." Are you capable of speaking a simple statement that doesn't sound like a text message? Do you find yourself writing work-related documents and spelling "you're" as "ur"?

The words "say," "said," and "told me" have been all but excised from American conversational English, and a new form of expression has stealthily infiltrated our culture. Here is an example of this absurd trend:

> "I asked Jim if he plans to drive or fly to the conference. He **goes**, 'I'd fly, but I'm short of cash.' Then I asked him if his firm doesn't pay for his transportation, and **he's all**, 'They should, but they don't.'"

There is only so much of "I *seen* this movie the other day..." or "...so I *says*..." *or* "...*and he goes*" that can be excused before these statements become symptoms of much larger problems; those of ignorance and laziness. A sizable percentage of our young people have English skills that reflect a most unintelligent "style," if you will, of communication. This is true even among educated individuals. Comparatively recently, statements are more often verbalized as questions, and verb tenses seem to have very little meaning. People earning extremely high salaries have vocabularies replete with mindless buzzwords and euphemisms.

Clichés

If you are going to use a cliché to remark on a situation or to add colorful commentary to a conversation, **please know what the damn maxim is**! I cannot tell you how many times I have heard statements like, "Well, that's just a horse of a different shade" or "That's the way the cupcake crumbles" or

NOTES

"A bird in the hand is better than nothing." When it comes to clichés, generally, less is more.

Quotes

If an Evolved Man quotes a famous person or recites a well-known saying, he follows two rules of guidance: 1) Know the quote, and 2) Know the source and credit it; don't pass it off as your own.

Vocabulary

Evolved Men are always on the look-out for new words and their meanings. By extending their vocabulary—whether industry-specific or general knowledge—Evolved Men also expand their capacity to communicate effectively.

Vulgarity

An Evolved Man possesses a wide vocabulary, from conservative to inspirational to offensive. (Regarding one's vocabulary: Building a vocabulary is a never-ending endeavor; it isn't something that can ever be 'finished'. Expect to continue building your vocabulary for the rest of your life.) While inappropriate for first dates, job interviews, and meeting future in-laws (among other times too numerous to count), profanity definitely has a place in today's modern culture. Timing is critical, but expletives used properly can be very descriptive—even comforting. Studies have shown that in tight-knit groups of mixed gender (work groups, friends, organization, and clubs), using profanity actually broke the stiff aura of formality, and enabled the group to create a closeness and trust that had been previously unattainable. Used inappropriately, however, profanity is distasteful at best, and a reason to deny your home loan, at worst. Evolved Men know to restrict the use of profanity to the times when they're in the company of their family,

NOTES

their friends, or their trusted associates (as some studies have proven that swearing in the workplace can actually promote better team collaboration).

Other vulgarities—gestures, noises, or body actions—I suppose can be termed as "communication," but are not needed or wanted by the woman in an Evolved Man's life. Those parts of "masculinity" must be left behind.

Spelling

Evolved Men proofread their writing, and know to be wary of the treasonous computer spellchecker. A misspelled and/ or mispronounced word can make the difference between writing a chronicle on "The Public Life of Pope John Paul II," or "The *Pubic* Life of Pope John Paul II." Of course, perfection is not possible (I wonder what spelling errors and typos will be found in this book despite all the editing and proofreading that has taken place), but effort is key.

Humor

All Evolved Men have a few good jokes in their repertoire; some clean, some double-entendre, some dirty, some raunchy. It would also do some good to have a few tales (tall or otherwise) for the children one encounters in life's travels.

E-mail and Instant Messages

E-mail is, in its simplest terms, "typed communication delivered in a hurry". I'm sure you are well aware that it's the most pervasive form of abbreviated communication. Favored acronyms and emoticons of today's high-tech culture are great for instant messages, but are unprofessional in business e-mail. It all comes down to audience. But as a constant, Evolved Men always proofread before they hit "Send." After all, spellcheckers only catch a percentage of typos and

NOTES

grammatical errors. If a word is spelled correctly but doesn't belong in the sentence, the spellchecker will not catch that error.

Conversation and Small Talk

Knowing what to say and when to say it is a combination of 50% talent and 50% experience. (Note: Experience is defined here as "mistakes one learns from".) When joining in a conversation, Evolving Men should be sure they are familiar with the subject matter, or should listen more than they speak. Asking questions about information that's new to you shows intelligence—not ignorance.

Evolved Men are aware of the following general rules for conversation when they are among close cohorts, or business associates. This kind of advice may sound basic and trite to you, but there are many men who simply don't have this information. That's why we have words and expressions like: blowhard, egomaniac, "he loves to hear his own voice", etc. Evolving Men-in-the-know, please take the following information with the proverbial grain of salt:

- If the speaker has the floor, don't one-up them with a story of your own. Let them have center stage.

- When engaging in conversation with someone you've just met, break the ice by being the first to speak. Recent news, hobbies, sports and the like are not incendiary topics, and will most likely start a friendly banter. Your views on death, taxes, politics, religion, and other controversial issues will definitely spark conversation, but you may find the tête-à-tête ending abruptly if opinions differ. Stay on the path to Evolution; start with light subject matter.

NOTES

- Should there be a lull in the conversation, encourage others to join in by offering a bit of previously unknown information that isn't an actual "topic"; for example: "Doug, didn't you just get back from Greece?"

- Be cognizant of the group you are in, and how they converse. Also note that the use of jargon will leave some people completely in the dark. Know your audience.

- When engaging in any conversation—or joining a discussion that's already in progress, there are two vital reasons to listen more than you speak: 1) When responding, you will have heard the other comments clearly and can articulate an intelligent response; be it a comment or a request for information. 2) There is always someone who knows more than you do. Learn at every opportunity.

<u>FASHION</u>

Today's Man's Man seems to be satisfied with his complete lack of style. The poor selection of clothing seen in the professional world and at social gatherings is offensive to the most mildly-cultured person. For those in the un-know: flip-flops are for the beach, ripped undergarments must be thrown away, and damn it—*please* know when a gathering is casual enough for cargo pants.

Evolved Men have a wardrobe (not a bunch of clothes) that speaks to style in the latest trends. (Not *fads*; **trends**. A trend is sustained movement; a fad is a momentary flash-in-the-pan.). If the 80s have called and want their parachute pants back, buying a few items to accent your current wardrobe is not the answer. Time to start over.

NOTES

Building a proper wardrobe is not unlike amassing a collection of music; it must be eclectic, rooted in basics, yet up-to-date—and provide an air of personal style that's appropriate to the event, location, and time of year. It is recommended that beginners visit higher-end department stores to gain knowledge; not only to be aware of the latest fashion trends, but also to get ideas that will help you create your own personal style. Once you've acquired some basic knowledge and have defined your own personal style, you may choose to personally visit specialty boutiques, as well as view their catalogues online—depending on how into fashion you are.

As a brief aside: I have observed a major decline in men's appearance over the past 10 years. I'm referring to guys I see at parks, nightclubs, schools (higher education, as well as young men in elementary schools), and when they're out shopping. They dress—in a word—**awfully**. Casual clothes can look very nice without being designer clothes. Nothing like wearing colors that go together, I always say. Is there actually something wrong with jeans that are hemmed to the right length, and fitted to their waist—or their hips? Please... sloppy is not a "style".

The Basics

Basic clothing can double for business/casual as well as a dressed-down look. In addition to staple items (underwear, casual jeans, relaxed-looking shirts), be sure to snap up items that can work with your lifestyle, your budget, and your body type. Basic black slacks, khakis, button-down shirts, a good pair of jeans, and/or three-button pullovers are safe for any occasion—conservative enough for dinner, casual enough for lounging.

NOTES

For Work

In many industries (many, but not all), the times of abiding by a mandatory dress code—power suit with a power tie—are gone. However, as an Evolved Man, looking dapper and stylish is important for self-esteem, for one's image in the workplace, and for future advancement. It isn't necessary to foolishly spend large sums of money, because a work wardrobe that's planned correctly can double as party/casual wear in most circumstances. Coordination and proper accessorizing are key.

Suits

In general, men shorter than 5'8" should avoid wearing double-breasted suits. Quite simply, it makes us (yes, us... I'm 5'5") look shorter. A single-breasted suit is perfect. Men over 5'8" should invest in a double-breasted suit... but your specific body build will dictate the best suit selection. Color varies according to the event, your profession, and your skin tone. However, most business professionals have a selection of dark suits (gray, black or blue) that are perfect for any occasion. Lighter colors are better for informal events/casual dates.

Shirts

An Evolved Man's wardrobe should include a wide variety of business-formal, business-casual, and informal shirts (with climate, season, and location taken into consideration). Long-sleeve button-up solids are fundamental for pairing with a suit, and if you wear a tie, make sure the color(s) go well with the shirt and the suit. And let's get this on the record: Leave the short-sleeves/suit combination in the 1950s where they belong.

NOTES

Sweaters

Sweaters—pullover, sleeveless, or cardigan styles—are a necessity in cooler climates. When making your choices, move beyond the solids (a la Mr. Rogers), and consider patterns. A pullover sweater can transform traditional informal slacks, and act as a dressier version of casual Fridays.

For Recreation

An Evolved Man's casual wear should always be just a touch on the fringe, but never outrageous or loud. Creating the right mood and image whether you're on a date, at a public social event, or entertaining at home —takes a careful balance. Be sure to pay attention to combinations that complement each other.

A basic casual-wear wardrobe should be varied, and should include everything from cotton pants and linen shirts, to solid silk tops (both pullover and button-up), to leather pants and/or vests (for the more extreme nightclub-faithful). Color and style that conform to current trends must be considered. In today's subculture, retro-wear is more a staple than a statement, so your fashion sense should reflect that. Brighter, bolder colors are certainly in order, and often in short supply in boutique shops; plan accordingly.

For more social-but-dressed occasions, a business suit with a relaxed shirt (collared, turtleneck, or mock turtleneck) is really all you need. For those wishing to make more of a fashion statement, a nominal investment in a suit with a Nehru jacket (a long narrow jacket with a stand-up collar) will provide the impetus for conversation, and garner sufficient retro-style points, too.

Athletic Gear

Whether attending a Yoga class, playing racquetball, or lifting weights, proper attire is important. After all, Evolved Men

NOTES

work out to improve the body *and the mind*; one element of that workout is nurturing a healthy self-image. Evolved Men should be able to walk by a mirror and see a healthy man who looks refreshed and invigorated; not a guy who looks like he just rolled out of bed.

When working out alone, a pair of loose-fitting sweats and a T-shirt or tank top is all that's needed. In a group setting, however, the rules change a bit. Coordinated workout clothing shows that you care as much about what covers the outside of your body, as you do for your body itself.

Footwear

Wearing worn, dilapidated shoes show a complete lack of self-respect,. Evolved Men recognize that what covers their feet is an important measure of style, coordination, and completeness, and should have a minimum of six pairs of shoes at their disposal: Basic black *and* brown dress shoes for business or pleasure, a decent pair of sandals, athletic shoes (for workouts), old athletic shoes or work boots, and a pair of flip-flops. All shoes should be in good condition, buffed to a shine (if applicable), and be appropriate for the atmosphere in which they are worn.

It should also be noted that an Evolved Man has a selection of belts that matches his shoes. Women match shoes and purses, Evolved Men match shoes with belts. Brown and black conservative (one each) are the bare minimum, although you should have a spare of each—and at least one casual belt.

Neckties

In conservative corporations, white-collar workers wear ties. (duh!) Start-up companies may allow jeans and a T-shirt in the office, however recent fashion trends show a "recycling effect" from times past... and the tie is wending its way

NOTES

back into pop and professional cultures. And besides, ties never lose their cool. Therefore, proficiency in proper tying is essential.

It is important to mention that the Four-in-Hand and the Half-Windsor are casual styles, and are the most common methods of tying a tie. Because this section has been written with a specific emphasis on style and elegance, those methods were not included.

How to Tie a Full (Double) Windsor

1. Put the tie around the back of your neck so that the wide end h a n g s down on the side of your dominant hand, a little more than twice

as low as the thin end. Wrap the wide end once around the thin end a few inches below your neck, pulling the wide end toward the side of your dominant hand.

2. Slip the wide end through the front of the V shape made by the knot, pulling it out toward the side of your dominant hand.

3. Wrap the wide end around the front of the knot.

4. Slip the wide end through the back of the V shape made by the knot.

5. Tuck the wide end into the front loop of the knot.

6. Pull down gently on the wide and thin ends from below the knot until the knot is tight.

7. Grasp the thin end and slide the knot up to your neck. If the thin end hangs lower than the wide end, untie the tie and begin again with the wide end hanging lower than it did the first time. If the wide end hangs too low, untie the tie and begin again with the wide end hanging higher than it did the first time. Persistence works…

How to Tie a Bow Tie

1. Adjust the length of the tie to fit your neck size. Lift up your collar and put the tie around your neck with the ends hanging down in front. One end should hang about one and one-half inches lower than the other.

2. Bring the longer end across, behind, and over the shorter end.

3. Pull the longer end under the shorter end forming a simple knot. Pull the knot snugly around your neck.

4. Fold the shorter end where the hourglass shape begins to narrow forming a bow shape. The bow shape should be in front. Hold the bow in a horizontal position at your neck.

NOTES

5. Bring the longer end over and in front of the shorter end.

6. Fold the longer end where the hourglass shape begins to narrow, forming a second bow. Bring the second bow under the first bow.

7. Tuck it into the space behind the first bow and pull snugly.

8. Adjust the shape of the two bows. Note: Bowties are not tied very tightly, and as such are re-tied throughout the evening or event.

How to Tie an Ascot

An ascot is a combination of a scarf and a tie, and has dropped somewhat from the fashion scene; but Evolved Men are encouraged to dare to be different.... so to each their own in this case.

1. Pull the ascot around the back of your neck as you would a tie. Let the left end hang slightly more than two inches longer than the right.

2. Wrap the left end over and around the right.

3. Continue around to complete a second turn.

4. Push the left end up, through the neck loop, so that it emerges over the top.

5. Center the top flap so that it is the only visible portion of the ascot. Spread the sides slightly.

6. Undo the top button of your shirt and tuck the ends of the ascot inside.

Formal Wear

When the invitation states "Black-tie optional", the Evolved Man know that "optional" means "mandatory." If you must rent a tuxedo, plan ahead and be sure you have either accurate measurements (inseam, outseam, shoulders, chest, and arm length), or personally speak with a quality fitter at the rental

NOTES

store. When you decide to take the plunge and make a purchase, be sure you see a reputable tailor. If you've never been to a professional tailor before, expect to be asked to which side you "dress", and the only permissible answers are

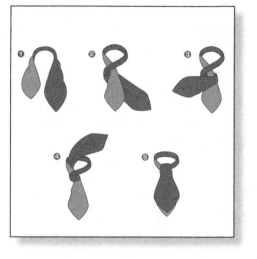

"right" or "left." (Believe me, they have heard all the one-liners in existence.)

A black-tie affair is not an opportunity to test out your new salmon-colored, wingtip-collared shirt. Save the fashion statements for the nightclub, and keep it simple. When it comes to formal, less can often be more and the conservative approach with a black cummerbund (worn pleats up!) or vest is the modus operandi.

"Unmentionables"

Evolved Men pay close attention to what touches their skin. Throw out any underwear that has tears or stains. Bottoms may be varied, depending on the activity. Sport trunks should be used for athletics only and shouldn't be worn under pants or slacks. Silk or linen boxers are the Evolved Man's choice, but those men not willing to fully embrace their feminine side may stick with generic briefs or boxers. Those who aren't mindlessly following some society-prescribed norms may decide to buy underwear that has a touch of mild daring. What you may think are outrageous designs and materials are probably not as shocking or as

NOTES

uncommon as you may think. An Evolved Man pursuing this course may find himself with a unique icebreaker when undressing for a woman.

It's mandatory to wear T-shirts, in whatever style you need—V-neck, crew neck, or tank. They protect against hideous sweat marks, and contribute to the longevity of your wardrobe. Please note: Undershirts are not outerwear, and should be replaced regularly.

As your inventory of underwear grows, there is a distinct possibility that the woman in your life will start "appropriating" items of choice, and as an Evolved Man, you should be prepared. You should not attempt to buy undergarments for her that are clearly styled for men, because what she wants are **yours**, not new ones from the store. Rather, you should always have a plentiful supply on hand. And although she may steal yours, you are not permitted to steal hers. (However, if your door swings that way, feel free to purchase your own. Not my style, but "different strokes for different folks" works just fine.)

Accessories

Certain accessories can change an outfit entirely, whereas others may only accent. When adding depth to a new or existing ensemble, pay close attention to colors, textures and styles.

For Cold Weather

As part of his wardrobe, an Evolved Man should have a pair of leather gloves, a hat, a scarf, a foldaway umbrella, and a raincoat—all in good repair. (Driving gloves are optional, but you might want to think about having the Porsche, MG, or convertible Prowler to match (he said sarcastically). Scarves and umbrellas should always be basic black, but colors of hats and overcoats may vary.

NOTES

Eyeglasses

If you wear eyeglasses, consider investing in three different frames styles: a conservative pair (metal), an informal pair (plastic or acrylic—which might showcase the fun-loving and unaffected part of your personality), and one for the sun (dark frames, dark tint).

Timepieces

A watch is one reflection of the self, and that self should change according to mood, clothing, and event and fashion trends. An Evolved Man should have different styles of watches in his fashion arsenal, and much like eyewear, both conservative and liberal timepieces are staples. Although pocket watches might be a bit inconvenient, the style points garnered by sporting one are considerable. A final note: Leave the calculator watches and the USB-connectable data watches for the tech geeks. But if you *are*, in fact, a geek, please wear yours proudly!).

Clothing Care

Now that you have an elegant, trendy wardrobe, you need to take care of it.

- Find a quality dry cleaner in your area. Request "light starch" for your dress and button-down shirts. A little starch helps in holding a tight fold at the collar, as well as a crease down the sleeves. Silk shirts, vests, and sweaters all need special care, so be sure to advise your cleaning professional of your needs.

- When performing the mind-numbing task of doing laundry, take the colors and weights of clothing into account. No more than four pair of jeans will come clean in a standard washer (regardless of what the manual says). Sort clothes by color, and if at all

NOTES

possible, invest in a water softener. Washing your clothes in soft water will get your clothes cleaner, which helps them last longer.

- Stains will usually come out if you act quickly when they happen. Club soda and a white rag are all you'll need if the unthinkable happens.

- Shoes should always be in good repair. Keep shoe polish on hand, and polish a minimum of three times a week (although nightly is best). Athletic shoes should be scrubbed after workouts. Holes in the soles mean they need to be repaired or replaced.

- Belts wear out. Be sure to replace worn or ripping belts.

- As an Evolved Man matures, there may be fluctuations in weight and/or waist size. Should you find yourself in the awkward position of wearing clothes that are tight around the mid-section, bite the bullet and visit the tailor. Wearing clothes that fit your body properly may actually hide your weight gain until the time you're able to do what's necessary to take the extra weight off. Should a weight-loss program not be an option, you will still feel quite comfortable, and look very well-dressed wearing tailored clothes.

- Stay in tune with trends and styles.

<u>HYGIENE</u>

A healthy human body sweats, exudes oil, sluffs off dead skin, loses at least 100 hairs a day, and smells foul unless it's cleaned on a frequent basis. Taking care of oneself is an important element of self-esteem, and fundamental to the

NOTES

creation of opportunities for a man to meet a woman... *and keep the relationship happy.*

Hygienic Protocol

- Earlier in the book, I told you some of the sad stories about how men commandeer the toilet, thereby setting the stage for women to be second-class citizens in their own homes. Now it's time to actually make a change. Let's finally end the toilet seat war. Be a gentleman, and put the seat down. There are many jokes made about this problem; jokes made by men, and laughed at by men. Pull it together, guys. Put the damn seat down and stop the subliminal control issues.

- Shave daily... even on the weekends. She wants to see you at your best, so don't save yourself only for work. (Exception: Men whose facial skin is tender and needs a break one day a week.)

- If the toilet paper is empty, replace it. It takes a total of three seconds.

- Aim. Aim. Aim.

- If you must read in the restroom, purchase a basket or magazine rack that fits next to the commode, and keep restroom visits under 10 minutes.

- Shower every morning. If your day was one of hard physical labor or you've just arrived home from a workout, shower prior to bedding down. Nothing is more disgusting than sharing a bed with a smelly body next to you.

NOTES

- Clip toenails in private, or even better, get a pedicure. If you clip them yourself, throw them in the trash when you're finished.

- Always wipe stray whiskers off the sink.

- Clean the mirror and the sink if you get toothpaste on them.

- Floss daily.

- Buy and use a facial scrub made for men.

- Buy and use hand and body lotion. It eliminates dry skin, and will add to your physical allure.

- Consult a scent expert and experiment with perfumes and colognes. It may sound ridiculous, but once you find one that suits your body chemistry, it will make all the difference.

- If you have wild eyebrows, pluck them, or seek the services of a men's spa.

- Visit the dentist at least once a year for a cleaning. Brown crusties (yuck!) are not endearing, and significantly contribute to mouth odor.

PHYSICAL FITNESS

Obesity in the United States has grown to epidemic proportions, and current national and international statistics show that there's no end in sight. It's now a common occurrence to see a high percentage of the male population hauling around spare tires hanging over their belts. The male attitude in general—"to just be what they are"—makes it

NOTES

114

clear that the double standard is (unfortunately) alive and well: Most of the men who have stopped (if they'd ever begun) stewarding the health and care of their bodies still expect the women in their lives to look like models.

I'm making an assumption, dear Reader: The fact that you're reading this book is excellent evidence of your discontent with the place you've been occupying in our society, to date. The vast variety of activities specifically designed to help men improve their physical condition and outward appearance are too numerous to list. The most important prerequisites for creating a physical metamorphosis are: 1) finding the activity that works for you, and 2) *commitment*. It really matters not which activity you choose… snowboarding, hiking, jogging, bodybuilding, 30 minutes of fast-paced walking, etc. Self-discipline… ***being consistent*** *is key.*

The most common and cost-effective method to get trim—and stay trim—is to join a health club. Good health clubs offer a wide range of amenities and membership options, to include: weights, cardiovascular workout equipment, racquetball, yoga, and there are even personal trainers. You'll have 24-hour access to endorphin highs, muscle building, and fat burning.

Keeping your body fit isn't *only* about appearance. Being physically fit also addresses a wide variety of important physical and mental needs: stress reduction, virility, digestion, vitality, and general mental defogging, just to name a few. Do it, and stick with it.

NOTES

Chapter VII:
Dating, Dining, And Sex

For an Evolved Man, dating is a more serious undertaking than it is for the average man. If your date is a woman who is pretty much on your wave-length, she'll most likely see you as a man who is friendly, understanding, funny, articulate, sensitive, and confident. No small feat. Following the guides I've presented on language, fashion, and literature, you will be a leg up on your competition... but there is more.

The Approach

When approaching a woman, sincerity is what matters. Believe this: The woman you are considering approaching has heard all the lines—it's time to invent a unique one: a truthful and straightforward one. A pleasant introduction is usually all that's necessary to get the ball rolling. ("Hi, I'm Alex and I wanted to come over and introduce myself. Your name is?") Simplicity and direct honesty sings to women, as they so rarely experience that approach from men.

NOTES

Unique Icebreakers

But there are times when much more effort is required. Some women don't give a man a chance to show that he may be an Evolved Man—smart, informed, and in tune with who they are. Some of the women I spoke with want to be swept off their feet. They want to be approached by someone who is charming, sincere, and above all... **unique**.

Here's one example from my life that illustrates the point:

> While my friends and I were driving down a crowded Silicon Valley street on a summer afternoon in the late 1980s, I couldn't help but notice a very striking young woman pulling up to a gas station pump. As she opened her car door and walked over to the pump, I was mesmerized. I slammed on my brakes, causing other cars behind me to do the same thing. Without really thinking, I hopped out of my car, and one of my friends slid over to the driver's seat. I sprinted across three lanes of moving traffic to get to her at the gas station! As you can well imagine, this caused a considerable commotion. By the time I got there, the woman was already doing her fill-up, while watching everything I did. As I approached her—panting, out of breath—I said, "You are just too beautiful to pump your own gas." This simple comment led to the exchange of telephone numbers. We dated frequently over the next few months.

Here's another:

> While walking along the upper level of a crowded mall in San Jose, California, I

NOTES

happened to look down at the people who were on the street level—and I saw an attractive woman shopping alone. I noticed that her ring finger was bare. I quickly took the stairs down to the flower shop, bought a single, thornless red rose, and wrote a card that read simply, "Dinner?" followed by my cell 'phone number. Attaching the card to the inside of the plastic wrapping, I returned to the upper level and waited patiently for her to pass below me. When she did, I gently dropped the rose over the side of the balcony, and watched as it landed a mere two feet in front of her. She picked it up, read the card, and looked up at me. I smiled, waved, and walked away. A couple of minutes later my cell phone rang, and we made arrangements to meet that evening.

Cool story. As I write, I smile… as I was only 20 years old.

Evolved Men: Get creative. Points for originality are granted on a first come, first-served basis.

Location, Location, Location

Once you have passed the introduction phase, you need to set the time and place for the first date. Venues for first dates should follow three basic guidelines: public, conservative, and casual. Meeting for coffee or a light lunch is perfect for a first date. If things don't work out, each of you are only out about an hour. As for the check, "going Dutch" is acceptable, but a sincere effort should be made to be the gentleman, and pay.

NOTES

Inspired Dates

Originality counts when dating. Whether you go for coffee, head to the beach and read poetry, or declare paintball war, romantic points are given to Evolved Men who plan, think, and stay focused on the date itself, not on what they want to happen at the conclusion of it. However, keep in mind: These dates are the standard by which your entire relationship will be measured as it matures. The trick is to set the bar high... and keep the bar high. Keep the spark and the passion alive.

Personal Account:

Many years ago, I called my then-girlfriend at work and asked her to get dressed up, as she was going to experience a night she would not soon forget. I picked her up in a rented convertible, blindfolded her, and told her we were headed down the Pacific Coast Highway for a surprise. I did allow short peeks, but for the bulk of the time she was in the dark (literally and figuratively).

Driving up the Pacific Coast was a ruse. We were actually going in circles for about 60 minutes. I stopped the car at a scenic hilltop. As we pulled up, a uniformed waiter appeared, opened her door, removed her blindfold, and announced, "Table for two? Right this way." He then led us to the top of the hill, and seated us at a candle-lit dinner table for two—complete with a strolling violinist.

NOTES

First Date Do's and Don'ts for Evolved Men

- Walk next to her, not a half-step in front of or behind her.

- Be kind and sensitive, not childish.

- Don't belch. Sometimes a person has to burp, and they then say 'excuse me'. But a belch is disgusting... and it only happens when a man is a pig.

- Don't order for her automatically; ask her what she wants, and then order for the two of you.

- Don't talk about past relationships.

- Don't discuss money, salaries, or sex.

- Don't use profanity.

- Ask before you hold her hand.

- Walk her to her car (or door). Shake hands with her, or kiss her hand when parting... unless she signals for more. Read the signs and stay a gentleman.

- Talk to her eyes, not her breasts or backside.

- Use cologne, but use it sparingly. A woman might want to experience the scent, but she definitely *does not* want to wear it herself.

- Eye contact, friendliness or flirting is not an automatic precursor to sex.

NOTES

- If you're married, you should treat every date with your wife like the first one.

DINING OUT

"Dining out" is much different than simply eating a meal outside the home. Dining is a sensual experience that has nothing to do with "going out to eat."

Reservations, Arrival, and Seating

When making reservations (which an Evolved Man makes well in advance of the date), be sure to note the name of the host/hostess who took your reservation when you check in. If you don't have reservations and try to squeeze your way in, it is extremely tacky to dangle cash in front of the maitre d'. Instead, discreetly palm the bill (minimum of $20) and whisper, "I'd appreciate anything you can do" and take a seat in the lounge.

When the time comes to be seated at the dining room table, the maitre d' will lead your special lady, and you'll be right behind her (holding the jacket you so smoothly relieved her of earlier).

Settings and Utensils

The place setting used for formal dining can be confusing, but knowing the correct utensil to use for each course of the meal is easy… once you're shown how. In general, the mode of operation is to work from the outside inward throughout the meal. To begin, your food server

NOTES

places your napkin in your lap immediately upon your being seated. Let's work our way around the setting as the meal progresses.

A. Napkin

B. Service Plate

C. Soup Bowl

D. Bread Plate with Knife

E. Water Glass

F. Red Wine Glass

G. White Wine Glass

H. Salad Fork

I. Dinner Fork

J. Dessert Fork

K. Knife

L. Teaspoon

M. Soup Spoon

Poor Service or Bad Food

If at any time restaurant service is poor, do not make a scene. Leave the table to find the manager. That way, he/she has an opportunity to rectify the problem while it's in progress. Also, note that stiffing your server will not get your point across; it will simply make you look cheap. Find the manager and discuss the problem. If the food itself was bad, discuss it with your server and the manager, and be sure to leave a tip. After all, the wait staff didn't prepare the food.

Notes

SEX

Sex is great. But sex—without knowing what to do and when to do it—is usually only pleasurable for the man. Evolved Men are careful to plan accordingly. A single kiss is not foreplay. Asking politely for oral sex will not get your request granted, and a brusque order won't be met with success, either. "Forceful sex" is not the same as "violent sex." Evolved Men have learned to put a woman's needs in the bedroom ahead of their own, and it is this consideration that leads to openness, trust, and complete reciprocity.

Preparation

Before engaging in any sexual act (unless the passion in the back seat of that taxi overwhelms both of you), take the time to clean up. A long shower alone (read: separately) will add to the anticipation and allow complete exploration. Follow your shower with a *light* touch-up of lotion.

You should never have to search for a condom. It should be discreetly available; **be smooth**. Evolved Men should be adept at unwrapping and putting on condom with one hand, and in under 10 seconds. Any longer and you are risking a mood-kill. If you can't do it, practice.

Venues

Ambiance is crucial to creating the vibes that make her want you, and occasionally varying the location and atmosphere will add to her passion. Candles and rose petals leading from the front door to the bed can be perfect. Don't knock that idea until you've tried it. Don't fall into the rut of predictability. Clearing the table—nude—after a seductive dinner can be passionate. The key here is reading her mood, and that comes with experience, experimentation, and above

NOTES

all, **listening**. Remember—it's contagious. What turns her on can't help but turn you on, too.

Kissing and Foreplay

A simple kiss is often the initial gauge by which women judge men. A sloppy, wet kiss is not usually well received, and slamming your tongue down her throat will also get a negative response. (Duh!) When engaging in foreplay, start gently. Let your hands and mouth wander as she allows, but pay attention to her responses. Light strokes on her cheek, neck, and back get extra points, as men usually ignore these areas. At the beginning, a light caress is definitely recommended, and should give way to a harder touch and grip as foreplay continues. This is the warm-up, and if you pay attention, you will find that foreplay is not a delay to the "real thing." It's a pleasure *for both of you.* Timing is *everything* during foreplay. Hands, shoulders, tongues and breathing must be in perfect harmony to release a woman's uninhibited potential. Going too fast or too slow at the wrong times will negate any progress you have achieved. Start slowly, and stay slow enough to watch for signs that encourage more rapid movement and advances.

Afterglow

After the first round, it's time for a break, and the Evolved Man is there to set the post-coital event. Encourage her to relax while you get her a warm washcloth and a glass of wine or ice water. Soft touches and conversation will keep the mood going and start the transition to round two. Sleeping, immediate showers, or the proverbial rollover are not options (the exception: it's a work night).

But don't stop here. Move on... experiment...

NOTES

chapter VIII:
The Untold Secrets of
Successful Relationships

While writing this guide to becoming an Evolved Man, I have made a number of observations concerning both successful and now-defunct relationships. I thank you, dear Readers, for joining me on this journey. I hope you have discovered things about yourself and your loved one you never knew existed. Good luck with your newfound knowledge. In addition to all you have read thus far, my hopes and expectations are that you will find the following tips and quips informative and useful in your quest for making an important positive change in your life.

- A good housekeeper will keep a couple happy and organized.

- Get a digital video recorder (DVR) She can watch and you can record (or vice versa). It will save your marriage. (Most of the people I interviewed agreed on one thing: having a DVR curbed more

NOTES

arguments and fights in their household, and they had noticeably improved their relationships because of it.)

- An Evolved Man should **never** buy jewelry, perfume, or lingerie for another man's wife or girlfriend.

- Pocket essentials for all Evolved Men: pen, Band-Aids®, pocketknife, photographs of your significant other, your kids, and of your parents (stay grounded!)

- Never forget her birthday.

- Never forget your anniversary.

- Upon returning home, the first person you kiss should be your wife. Kids are the light of your lives together, but your wife should be #1.

- Turn off the TV, or fold up the newspaper, and make eye contact when you speak to her.

- Flowers every Friday make for magic weekends.

- Cooking together can lead to passion transferring from the stove to the bedroom (or dining table!).

- Don't be afraid to say, "I'm sorry," if it's a sincere feeling. False pride is part of the macho mentality. Don't be afraid to say, "I was wrong." You'll lose nothing. On the contrary: You'll both benefit.

- Never fight in public, or in front of children.

- Never call her names in anger. Once they leave your mouth, words of hate cannot ever be taken back. Forgiven, yes… but never taken back.

NOTES

- Stop blaming her for your shortcomings. They're *yours*, not hers.

- Never tell her she's fat. If she has a few pounds on her, it's *healthy*, not fat. If she's obese, encourage her to seek the advice of a health care professional.

- Say nice things about her to everyone you meet. Remember: You chose her to be in your life for those nice things. Tell the world!

- Never go to bed angry.

- If she cooks, you clean, and vice versa.

- Always trust her word.

- Encourage her.

- Enjoy her successes vicariously.

- Don't argue over bills. Cash comes and goes.

- Join a class together. You'll learn about the subject, and about each other, too.

- Tell her every day that you love her.

- Never take for granted that you are together. Love her like the first day you met.

- In the face of adversity, always be brave—even if you have to fake it. Bravery looks the same to the outside world whether it is real or imagined. The amazing part of faking bravery is that it very quickly becomes real, as your fear dissipates.

NOTES

- Always keep your promises. If life has intervened and keeping your promise is impossible, make sure you talk about it as soon as you know.

- Never say, "I can't." You might not be *able to* at this moment, but you can choose to learn.

NOTES

Appendix:
The Evolved Man's Gratuity Guide

An experienced, Evolved Man knows that service personnel are not salaried, and the gratuity is what counts. Keep in mind that tipping is discretionary, but an Evolved Man would never stiff anyone. If you were displeased with service, leave a smaller tip—and have a chat with a supervisor or manager. Be mindful that service professionals are human beings; they have good and bad days just like the rest of us. Having enough for the bill but not enough for the tip is unacceptable. The gratuity is part of the experience and should be part of your budget considerations.

Bars, Grills and Restaurants

- Food server – minimum 20%

- Cocktail server - 15–20%

- Bartender - 15–20% or a minimum of $1 per drink. If you were waiting in the lounge before the meal, be sure to settle up with the bartender prior to dining.

NOTES

- Wine steward - 10% of the wine bill

- Maitre d' or Hostess - If he/she gets you a special table—or the restaurant is full and you had no reservation—a minimum of $20.

- Coat check - minimum $1 per coat (even if hung on the same hanger)

- Restroom attendant – minimum $1

- Musician in lounge – minimum $5, more if a request is played.

- Takeout – With good service, $2 or up to 10%.

Airport and Ground Transportation Personnel

- Porter or skycap – minimum $3 per bag... more, if the bags are heavy. $5 extra for curbside check-in. If you arrive late and he helps you get to your flight on time, tip an extra $20.

- Taxi, limo, or shuttle, driver - 15% of the total fare. Up to 20% if the driver helps with the bags or makes extra stops.

- Driver of courtesy shuttle – minimum $2 + $1 per bag

Lodging

- Valet Parking Attendant – minimum of $2 when the car is returned to you

NOTES

- Doorman – Cab hailing – minimum $2 Bag handling - $2 per bag Metro information – Discretionary, but a minimum of $10

- Bellman - Bag handling - $2 per bag

- Concierge - $20 for help with hard-to-get dinner reservations or theater tickets. Tipping is optional for basic advice.

- Housekeeping - $3 per day (left on pillow each morning)

Wedding Services

- Civil ceremony officials – minimum $50

- Minister, priest, rabbi - minimum of $100 (given by the Best Man following the ceremony)

- Limo driver - 12% of the total fare

- Coat check - $1 per guest

- Photographers - up to 15% as merits outstanding service

- Musicians/Disc Jockey - up to 15% as merits outstanding service

- Wedding soloist – minimum $50

- Reception – Open Bar: $1 per drink

NOTES

Barbers and Stylists

- Barber - $5 minimum (more if a shave is included)

- Hair Stylist/Color Specialist – 10% of the total bill

- Shampooer (or other assistant) - $5 each.

- Manicure, Pedicure, or Facial – minimum 15%

Casino Dealers

- Cards/Craps dealer – 20% table value per session (e.g., on a $25 blackjack table, the tip is $5)

- Poker dealer - 10% of your winnings (but not to exceed $100).

- Roulette dealer - 20% of the table value per session

- Keno runner – minimum $2 per ticket; 5% of winnings

- Cocktail waitress - $1 per drink, minimum.

Holiday Tipping for...

- Maid - One week's pay, minimum

- Mail Carrier - $20 (as per Federal cap on gifts)

- Doorman - $50 minimum

- Manicurist/Pedicurist - $25 minimum

NOTES

- Hairdresser/Stylist - $25 minimum

- Teacher - Gift valued at $50

- Baby Sitter - Three night's pay

- Full-Time Nanny - Two week's pay

- Daycare Professional - $100 plus a gift valued at $50

- Newspaper Delivery - $20

NOTES

Acknowledgements and References

There are many people to thank: the women and men who trusted me and allowed me to peek at...delve into...analyze their relationships, my wife, my kids, my mother, and so many others who helped me along the way. I also want to refer to a skeleton list of quality books written by some very forward-thinking, insightful, and talented authors. I would recommend these to anyone on their Evolutionary journey—any man or woman learning to choose a healthier and happier life path.

Find out more at theproblemwithwomenismen.com

- Keen, S. 1992 *A Fire in the Belly*. Bantam.

- Hirshman, L. 2006. *Get To Work: A Manifesto for the Women of the World*. Viking Adult.

- Toffler, A. 1970 *Futureshock*. Bantam.

- Hirsch, E. D., J. Kett, J. Trefil. 2002. *The New Dictionary of Cultural Literacy*. Houghton Mifflin.

NOTES

- Tsu, S., and T. Cleary. 2005. *The Art of War.* Shambhala.

- Seguin, F. 1998. *Le Language des Fleurs*, Editions du Chene.

NOTES

Made in the USA
Coppell, TX
04 December 2019